llieatre

Live Theatre
presents the world premiere of

Inheritance

by Mike Packer

Wednesday 3 to Saturday 27 November 2010

The play was commissioned by and first performed
at Live Theatre, Newcastle upon Tyne

A word from the writer

The two most precious things my dad left behind were a set of values and a sense of humour. He also tried to leave his council house by dumping lifelong principles and exercising his 'right to buy' when he knew the end was in sight. But luckily, my siblings and I were saved from each other and the credit crunch by a lack of familial fiscal credibility – even in those not so long ago days when banks were throwing money at anyone who drew breath.

When he died I felt an overwhelming desire to try and be a better person. To take on some of the qualities and values that he personified. I'm sure that this is a common feeling when a parent dies. As is a sharper awareness of lineage, family history, one's own mortality, and what thing of real value one might pass on to one's own children.

This play springs from that well. And the questions posed are simple – What is of true value? How should we behave whilst we are here?

Mike Packer

With thanks to: Theatre Royal Stratford East, Soho Theatre, Kerry Michaels, Matthew Xia, Nina Steiger, Eddie Darke, John Tomaney and Tyne Cruises.

Inheritance

BY **Mike Packer**

Cast (in order of appearance)

David Hargreaves Harry
Matthew Wait Frank
Steven Hillman Terry
Melanie Hill Los
Martina Laird Susan

Creative & Production Team

Mike Packer Writer
Lisa Goldman Director
Ben Stones Designer
Philip Gladwell Lighting Designer
Matt McKenzie Sound Designer
Paul Aziz AV Design
Fight Director Bret Yount
Carolann Crawford Dialect Coach
Lucy Jenkins CDG and Sooki McShane CDG Casting

For Live Theatre

Lou Duffy Costume Supervisor
Emma Roxburgh Assistant Director
Drummond Orr Production Manager
Paul Aziz Stage Manager
Kate McCheyne Deputy Stage Manager
Heather Robertson Deputy Stage Manager
Dave Flynn Technical Manager
Mark Tolan Technician
Max Roberts Artistic Director
Gez Casey Script Advisor
Jim Beirne Chief Executive
Wendy Barnfather Operations Director

Cast

David Hargreaves Harry

David's theatre credits include: *Pub Quiz is Life* (Hull Truck), *The Cordelia Dream* (RSC at Wilton's Music Hall), *The Taming of the Shrew* (RSC), *Puntila* (Belgrade Theatre), *On the Shore of the Wide World* (Royal Exchange & National Theatre), *The Hypochondriac* (Belgrade Theatre), *King Lear* and *Romeo and Juliet* (RSC), *The Changing Room* (Royal Court) as well as seasons with Birmingham Rep, Moving Theatre, Glasgow Tron, Nottingham Playhouse, Leeds Playhouse, Sheffield Crucible, Soho Theatre, Bush Theatre, Old Red Lion, Young Vic, Foco Novo and Riverside Studios.

Television credits include: regular appearances in *Mersey Beat*, *Making Out* (BBC), *Albion Market* (Granada), *Bloomin' Marvellous* (DL Taffner), *Strangers* (Granada), *Headmaster* (BBC), *Sorry I'm a Stranger* (Thames), as well as episodes of *The Bill* (Thames) *Casualty* (BBC), *Heartbeat* (YTV), *Peak Practice* (Carlton TV), *Bergerac* (BBC), *Ruth Rendell* (Blue Heaven Productions), *Harry* (Union Pictures), *Poirot* (LWT), *Minder* (Thames) and *Professionals* (LWT).

Film credits: *Agatha* (Sweetwall/First Artists/Warner Bros.), *Othello* (HBO) and *She's Been Away* (BBC).

Matthew Wait Frank

Matthew Wait trained at Rose Bruford School of Speech and Drama.

Matthew's theatre credits include: *Some Explicit Polaroids*, *A State Affair* and *Rita, Sue & Bob Too* (Out of Joint), *Bad Company* (Bush Theatre), *Weldon Rising* (Royal Court), *Birdy* (Lyric Hammersmith & West End) and *Tartuffe* and *Certain Young Men* (Almeida Theatre). Most recent theatre credits include *Piranha Heights* (Soho Theatre) and *Mixed Up North* (Out of Joint).

Matthew's television credits include: *Clarissa* (Acorn Media), *Crocodile Shoes* (Red Rooster/BBC), *Out of the Blue* (BBC), *Sam Saturday* (Cinema Verity), *Young Indiana Jones* (Amblin Entertainment/Lucasfilm/Paramount), *Pie in the Sky* (BBC), *99:1*, *Where the Heart Is* (Anglia Television), *Wing and a Prayer* (Thames), *Submerged* (NBC Studios/Once Upon a Time Films), *Inspector Lynley*, *Heroes & Villains* and *Silent Witness* (BBC) and *The Tudors* (Peace Arch Entertainment). Matthew also played series regular 'Luke' in *Casualty* (BBC). Most recent credits include guest appearances in *Coronation Street* (Granada) and *Heartbeat* (YTV).

Steven Hillman Terry

Steven's theatre credits include: *Fair* and *Once Upon A Time In Wigan* (Contact Theatre, Manchester) and a tour of *The Fifteen Streets*.

Steven's recent television credits include: *Coronation Street* (Granada), *Casualty* (BBC), *Emmerdale* (Granada) and *Inspector George Gently* (BBC). He has also appeared on screen in *Heartbeat* (YTV), *Shameless* (Channel 4), *The Royal* (YTV), *The Red Riding Trilogy* (Revolution Films), *Steel River Blues* (ITV), *Gifted* (ITV/Rollem Productions), *See No Evil – The Moors Murders* (Granada), *The Street* (ITV), *Buried* (Channel 4), *Donovan* (Granada) and *The League of Gentlemen* and *Clocking Off* (BBC).

Steven has also appeared in films *The Bait Room* (Benchmark Films) directed by Vincent Woods and *Somers Town* (Tomboy Films) directed by Shane Meadows.

Melanie Hill Los

Melanie's theatre credits include: *Maggie's End* (Shaw Theatre), *Tongue of a Bird* (Almeida Theatre), *Cardiff East* (Royal National), *I Have Been Here Before* (Royal Exchange), *Women Beware Women* (Royal Court) and *Educating Rita* (British American Theatre Institute).

Television credits include: *Candy Cabs* (Splash Media), *Joe Maddison's War* (Mammoth Screen), *The Thick Of It*, *Holby City* and *Rather You Than Me* (BBC), *White Girl* (Tiger Aspect), *The Street II* (ITV Productions), *Cape Wrath* (Ecosse TV Productions), *Emmerdale* and *Hot Money* (Granada), *Playing The Field* (Tiger Aspect), *Crocodile Shoes* (Red Rooster/BBC), *Finney* (Zenith), *Bread* (BBC) and *Auf Wiedersehen Pet* (Central).

Film credits include: *Break The Fall* (Stone City Films), *Stardust* (Paramount), *Brassed Off* (Prominent Features/Channel 4) and *When Saturday Comes* (Capitol Films).

Martina Laird Susan

Martina's recent theatre credits include: *All The Little Things We Crushed* (Almedia Theatre), *Bad Blood Blues* (Theatre Royal Stratford East), *Othello* (Donmar Warehouse), *The Five Wives of Maurice Pinder* (National Theatre), *Arabian Knights* (West End & international tour), *Breath Boom* (Royal Court), *Hyacinth Blue* (Clean Break) and *The White Devil*, *Three Hours After Marriage* and *Troilus and Cressida* (RSC).

Television credits include: *Shameless* (Channel 4), *Free Agents* (Big Talk Productions Ltd), *Casualty* (BBC), *Touch of Frost* (ITV), *The Bill* and *Wing and a Prayer* (Thames), *Jonathan Creek* (BBC), *The Governor* (La Plante Productions), *Little Napoleans* (Picture Palace) and *Eastenders* (BBC).

Film credits include: *Blitz* (Blitz Films/Lionsgate), *For-Get-Me Not* (Quicksilver Films) and *The Hurting* (Fluid Films Productions).

Creative & Production Team

Mike Packer Writer

Previously an actor, Mike worked extensively in theatre and television. As a performance poet he was crowned London slam champion, and played the pyramid stage at Glastonbury.

His first play, *To Live Like a King* was runner up for the Allied Domecq New Playwrights Award. Subsequent plays, *Card Boys*, *A Carpet, a Pony & a Monkey*, and critically acclaimed *The Dysfunckshonalz!* all premiered at Bush Theatre. In 2011 *The Dysfunckshonalz!* will open in The West End and is also to be a film.

Lisa Goldman Director

Lisa is a director and writer who until recently was Artistic Director of Soho Theatre where she directed world premieres *Behud* (also at Coventry Belgrade), *Shraddha* (winner of 2010 Meyer Whitworth Award), *Everything Must Go* – theatre's first response to economic crisis, *This Isn't Romance* (winner of 2007 Verity Bargate Award; directed for Radio 3's The Wire), *Piranha Heights* and *Leaves of Glass* by Philip Ridley, *Baghdad Wedding* (winner of the 2008 George Devine Award and Meyer Whitworth Awards; also directed for Radio 3 Sunday play), *A Couple of Poor* and *Polish-Speaking Romanians* (also co-translated). Previously as Artistic Director of the Red Room, world premieres included writing and directing the site-specific *Hoxton Story*, *The Bogus Woman* (Fringe First and Manchester Evening News Awards - Bush Theatre, Traverse Theatre, international tour & Radio 3 Sunday play), *Made in England*, *Sunspots, Surfing*, *Obsession* (all Time Out Critics Choice seasons at BAC) and producing *The Censor* and *Stitching* (Royal Court and Bush Theatre - both won Time Out Live Awards for best production).

Ben Stones Designer

Ben trained in stage design at Central Saint Martins College of Art & Design and went on to win a Linbury prize commission to design *Paradise Lost* for Rupert Goold.

Designs include: *Creditors* (Donmar Warehouse, Harvey Theatre BAM New York), *Kiss Of The Spider Woman* (Donmar Warehouse & national tour), *Paradise Lost* (Headlong Theatre), *Beautiful Thing* (Sound Theatre, Leicester Square), *The Arab Israeli Cookbook* (Tricycle Theatre), *The Mighty Boosh*, *Mitchell and Webb Live!* and *Pappys Fun Club* (Phil McIntyre national tour), *When Five Years Pass* (Arcola Theatre), *The Herbal Bed* and *The Real Thing* (Salisbury Playhouse), *Taste of Honey* and *Salt* (Royal Exchange), *Romeo and Juliet* (Shakespeare's Globe), *My Mother*

Said I Never Should (Watford Palace), *My Dad's a Birdman* (Sheffield Crucible), *Speaking in Tongues* (Duke of Yorks, West End), *Crocodile* (Frank McGuinness premiere for Sky Arts), *Ingredient X* (Royal Court), *Doctor Faustus* (Royal Exchange) and *An Enemy of the People* starring Antony Sher (Sheffield Crucible).

Philip Gladwell Lighting Designer

Philip's theatre credits include: *The Bodies* (Live Theatre), *Love The Sinner* (National Theatre), *Miss Julie* (Schaubhune - Berlin), *Five Guys Named Moe* (Theatre Royal Stratford), *After Dido* (English National Opera), *My Romantic History* (Bush Theatre & tour), *1984* and *Macbeth* (Royal Exchange), *Punk Rock* (Lyric Hammersmith & UK tour), *Terminus* (Abbey & international tour), *Once on This Island* (Birmingham Rep), *Harvest* (UK tour), *Amazonia*, *Ghosts*, *The Member of the Wedding* and *Festa!* (Young Vic), *Oedipus Rex* (Royal Festival Hall), *Oxford Street* and *Kebab* (Royal Court), *Il trittico* (Opera Zuid), *Testing the Echo* (Out of Joint), *Falstaff* (Grange Park Opera), *Daisy Pulls it Off*, *Blithe Spirit* and *Black Comedy* (The Watermill), *Low Pay? Don't Pay* (Salisbury Playhouse), *Dandy in the Underworld*, *Shradda*, *Overspill*, *HOTBOI* and *Tape* (Soho Theatre), *Melody* and *In the Bag* (Traverse Theatre), *Mother Courage and Her Children* (Nottingham Playhouse & UK tour), *Bread and Butter* (Tricycle), *The Canterville Ghost* (Peacock), *Awakening* and *Another America* (Sadler's Wells).

Matt McKenzie Sound Designer

Born in New Zealand, Matt worked at Lyric Hammersmith before joining Autograph in 1984. He was Sound Supervisor for The Peter Hall Seasons (The Old Vic).

Recent credits include: *The Dysfunckshonalz!* (Bush Theatre), *Putting It Together*, *The Gondoliers*, *How to Succeed in Business Without Really Trying*, *Carousel*, *Babes In Arms*, *Funny Girl*, *Music Man* and *Oklahoma* (Chichester Festival Theatre), *Oh What A Lovely War*, *Sweeney Todd*, *Company*, *Into The Woods* and *Merrily We Roll Along* (Derby Playhouse), *The House of Bernarda Alba*, *Journey's End*, *Tango Argentino*, *Misery*, *Long Day's Journey Into Night*, *Macbeth*, *Sexual Perversity in Chicago*, *A Life in the Theatre*, *Swimming With Sharks*, *Nicholas Nickleby*, *Lysistrata*, *The Master Builder*, *A Streetcar Named Desire*, *Amadeus*, *Forbidden Broadway*, *Blues in the Night* and *Love Story* (West End), *Family Reunion*, *Henry V*, *Hamlet*, *The Lieutenant of Inishmore*, *Julius Caesar* and *A Midsummer Night's Dream* (RSC).

Emma Roxburgh Assistant Director

Emma trained in her native north east at the Live Northumbria Academy. As Assistant Director she has worked with Max Roberts (*RSC Testimonies*), Martin Wylde (*Five Kinds of Silence*), Steve Gilroy (*Home By Now*) and Deborah Bruce (*Mam, Dad, Monkey and Me* and *Scarborough*). As well as directing credits for Live's Youth Theatre, Emma has written and produced short films and community plays for young people.

About Live Theatre

From its base on Newcastle's quayside, Live Theatre produces work as varied and diverse as the audiences it engages with. To do this it:

• Creates and performs new plays of world class quality

• Finds and develops creative talent

• Unlocks the potential of young people through theatre

Founded in 1973, the theatre was recently transformed via a £5.5 million redevelopment. The result is a beautifully restored and refurbished complex of five Grade II listed buildings with state-of-the-art facilities in a unique historical setting, including a 160-seat cabaret style theatre, a studio theatre, renovated rehearsal rooms, a series of dedicated writer's rooms as well as a thriving café and bar.

www.live.org.uk

Mike Packer

Inheritance

faber and faber

First published in 2010
by Faber and Faber Limited
74–77 Great Russell Street, London WC1B 3DA

Typeset by Country Setting, Kingsdown, Kent CT14 8ES
Printed in England by CPI Bookmarque, Croydon CR0 4TD

A CIP record for this book
is available from the British Library

ISBN 978-0-571-27509-0

2 4 6 8 10 9 7 5 3 1

For Julz, Frank and Jake

Characters

Harry
seventy

Frank
his son, late forties

Terry
his son, fifty

Susan
Frank's wife, mid-forties

Lorraine (Los)
Terry's wife, mid-forties

INHERITANCE

In memory of Mick Packer
1923–2009

*The living room of a 1940s-built terraced house in Low
Fell, Gateshead, Tyne and Wear. The wallpaper is twenty
years old and corners hang loose. Photographs of family
life stretching back through generations adorn the walls
and sit on the mantelpiece above the defunct 1970s three-
bar electric fire. A hatch is cut into the wall, on the other
side of which is the kitchen. A small TV with a Sky box
sits on a 1970s wooden TV and video station. Opposite
this is Harry's armchair – battered, green, and comfortable.
Harry, seventy, stands in the centre of the room, eyes
closed, body jerking in rhythm to the music: Louis
Armstrong and Duke Ellington, 'Don't Get Around Much
Anymore'. He then throws in a bit of pretend trumpet,
a little dance with his partner, sings a couple of lines, and
fades the music with the remote.*

Harry I'm ready, Gracie. I'm ready, my love.

*He picks up the phone, hits a button, and a light
comes up on Frank, late forties, answering the call.*

Frank Hello . . .

Harry Frank . . .

Frank Hello, Dad, alright?

Harry Aye, fine. You?

Frank Yeah, fine, yeah.

Harry How are my boys?

Frank Fine, little bastards. They wake up at six, start
fighting at ten past, and stop fighting when they go to bed.

Harry That's natural.

Frank I know.

Harry Brothers.

Frank I was gonna bring them over this weekend but Suze is working . . .

Harry She's gotta take it while it's there.

Frank The week after. I'll make sure we get over then.

Harry Listen, er, I've, er, I've got some bad news . . . I've, er . . . Cancer, I've got cancer.

Beat.

Frank Right.

Harry It's okay. It's not that bad. I'm not gonna die. Not yet, anyway. (*Laughs.*) No, it's bowel cancer, I think they might have caught it in time. I've gotta see the specialist in a few weeks.

Frank A few weeks? You can't wait a few weeks. Let's go private, we'll pay.

Harry No, no, no. I wouldn't do that.

Frank Dad.

Harry I don't want t go private. I support the NHS.

Frank Dad, this isn't a time for principles.

Harry It's exactly the time for principles. Anyone can spout principles when they're not bein' tested.

Frank We'll pay for the initial consultation. Just to see where we are.

Harry I'm not barging someone else out of the way by flashing money.

Frank Dad . . .

Harry One more word on the subject and I'll hang up.

Frank Okay. Okay. Okay. Right. Okay, Dad, okay. To be honest, Dad, you know I'm not a fan of conventional medicine, anyway. What about – I know you're not a believer, but we know the most amazing healer.

Harry No.

Frank He'd just lay his hands on you.

Harry If he lays his hands on me, I'll lay my hands on him.

Frank Okay. Have it your way. Die when you don't have to. Go on, die. (*Pause.*) Sorry, Dad.

Harry Anyway, apart from that everything's okay.

Frank I love you, Dad.

Harry chokes up. Terry, fifty, wearing a Newcastle shirt, appears at the window, looks in, and knocks. Harry looks over. Terry goes to the front door.

Harry That's Terry, I'd better go.

Frank Have you told him yet?

Harry No. I'll tell him now.

A key turns in the lock and the front door opens.

Frank I'll come over at the weekend.

Harry You don't have to do that.

Frank I'll bring the kids.

Harry Just be normal.

Terry enters, picks up the TV remote, switches on Sky Sports News.

Frank I'm coming.

Harry I'd better go.

Frank I'll see you Sunday.

Harry Well . . . okay. That'd be lovely.

Frank Bye, Dad.

Harry Bye, son.

They hang up. Lights down on Frank.

Terry Who was that?

Harry Frank.

Terry Woman.

Pause.

Harry Er . . .

Terry I've been made redundant.

Harry What?

Terry I've been made redundant.

Harry What d'you mean, you've been made redundant?

Terry I've lost my job. What d'you think I mean?

Harry Why? What you done?

Terry Nothin'. They're downsizin'. I'm the odd man out.

Harry They can't do that.

Terry Well, they have.

Harry You've been there since school.

Terry So what?

Harry Just you?

Terry Just me.

Harry Why you?

Terry I dunno.

Harry You dunno?

Terry I dunno.

Harry They must have given you a reason?

Terry I don't drink. That's what it is. I don't drink.

Harry What d'you mean, you don't drink?

Terry I'm the only one who don't get pissed on a Friday night. Everyone else gets arseholed. I don't drink. That's what I mean.

Harry Who made that decision?

Terry The Head of Department.

Harry Who is he?

Terry What's it matter who he is? It's his job.

Harry What's his name?

Terry Bart.

Harry Bart?

Terry Simpson.

Beat.

Harry This isn't a joke. You have to learn to stand up for yourself. I can't do it for you for ever, you know. I won't be around for ever. What's the union say?

Terry The union? (*Laughs.*)

Harry What do they say?

Terry Unions are a joke nowadays.

Harry Who's your shop steward?

Terry Who cares?

Harry When I was at Leslie's . . .

Terry Shut up.

Harry D'you pay your subs?

Terry No choice.

Harry Well then. This is what a union's for.

Terry Not any more it's not.

Harry I'm ringin' Mickey Harris.

Terry Leave it.

Harry What's your steward's name?

Terry Roman.

Harry Roman?

Terry Abramovich.

  Beat.

Harry You've got kids. You can't take this lyin' down.

Terry I already have. It happened a month ago.

Harry What?

Terry I'm goin'. (*Heads for the door.*)

Harry Come back here.

  Terry stops. Beat.

Terry I dunno what to do, Dad. I've not told Los.

Harry I'm ringin' Mickey Harris.

Terry No.

Harry He owes me. I was his shop steward. I put him up for the area council. He loves me. I'll sort this out.

Opens his address book and looks up Mickey's number.

He's always said, 'Harry, any problems, ring me.' (*Picks up the phone receiver.*)

Terry I took some money.

Harry What?

Terry I didn't mean to. It was on the table. I just took it.

Harry What money?

Terry Two hundred quid. It was just lyin' there and I took it.

Pause.

Harry It was just lyin' on the table?

Terry Aye.

Harry Was anyone around?

Terry It was Friday night. They'd all gone to the pub. I was sweepin' up. Puttin' the teas away. There it was. Two hundred quid.

Harry And you took it?

Terry Yeah. I forgot about the CCTV. I thought I'd got away with it.

Harry Whose was it?

Terry It was the whip for the piss-up. They'd left it behind. I'd just put it in my pocket and Dodge walked in, he was like, 'Where is it?' And I like, 'I dunno,' it just came out. I was thinkin' of takin' it over to 'em but I just said 'I dunno.' And once I'd said that I couldn't go back, could I?

Harry So they weren't downsizin'? You got the sack?

Terry Yeah.

Pause.

Harry You won't get another job as good as that.

Terry I know.

Harry You'll have to get some sort of job.

Terry I thought I'd do some mini-cabbin'.

Harry In your car?

Terry I've not got an MOT.

Harry You can't pick up passengers in a car with a hole in the floor.

Terry I know.

Harry What you talkin' about then?

Terry I dunno.

Pause.

Harry And you've not told Los?

Terry I thought I'd try and get another job first.

Harry I'll phone Dave. See if he's got a car you can cab in.

Terry I've asked him. He's got one I can have for fifteen hundred. I've not got it.

Harry What about your redundancy? They've got to pay you redundancy.

Terry I've had it. When the firm got took over we all signed it away for a lump sum. It was either that or the sack. They owed me tuppence-ha'penny, but they, you know – 'We'll prosecute,' so . . . It's finished, Dad. It's over. I'm out on my arse. I dunno what to do, Dad. I can't keep up. I'm crackin' up. I dunno what I'll do.

Pause.

Harry I'll buy you the car.

Terry Can you?

Harry No, I can't. But I will. I've got credit cards. I'll use them.

Terry Thanks, Dad. I'll pay it off. I promise.

Harry I've heard that before.

Terry I will. On me life. I will.

Harry Go away. I'm tired. I wanna sleep.

Terry Thanks, Dad. Sorry.

Harry It's alright. Leave it with me.

Terry Cheers, Dad. Sorry.

Harry Forget it. It happens. Don't worry, son. We'll be alright.

Pause. Terry exits. Pause.

Harry What's he gonna do when I'm gone, Gracie? What's he gonna do?

Harry sighs, sits in his armchair, turns the TV off and Louis and the Duke back on. Fade to black.

SCENE TWO

Harry sits in his armchair. Frank enters with a glass of green juice.

Frank Carrot, spinach, broccoli, avocado, alfalfa, and a spoonful of spirulina.

Harry It looks like sewage. (*Takes the glass.*)

Frank It's really nice. Try it. You'll probably feel a bit of a 'rush' when you drink this.

Harry A rush?

Frank Yeah, you know, kind of a whoosh, 'let's go'. That's what I get. Honestly. And it's full of all the nutrients you're gonna need to fight off the radiotherapy.

Harry The cancer.

Frank The cancer, yeah. Honestly, you're gonna need every nutrient.

Harry takes a sip.

Harry Mmm. Lovely.

Frank So you know how to use the juicer, now?

Harry Yeah, got that.

Frank And I've left a list of all the ingredients for each juice.

Harry Good.

Frank But the only one you really need to have every day, there's a jug full in the fridge, is the colon cleanser.

Harry Lovely.

Frank We'll get there, Dad.

Harry I know, son.

Frank We'll beat this.

Harry I know, son.

Frank Drink up then.

Harry In my own time.

Frank Absolutely. Yeah. Right.

He delves into a carrier bag and takes out a very large aromatherapy candle.

Fantastic, these are. They change the atmosphere of a place completely. It kind of . . . harmonises, Dad. A sense of calm. And, I'll tell you what, I've got some Tibetan monk music you might want to listen to.

Harry I don't know about that.

Frank No, honestly, Dad, let me just put some on for you, see if you like it.

He takes a CD from the bag and holds it up for Harry to see.

The Dalai Lama, Dad. You know, I know you don't but – Honestly, just look at his face, he's . . . he's happy, isn't he? You should hear his laugh, Dad. Have you ever heard him laugh?

Harry No.

Frank Oh, Dad, honestly. It's the greatest laugh ever. It's infectious. It must be on a tape somewhere. I'll tell you what, I'll get it for you. If the whole world heard him laughing, they'd be laughing too. I wish I had a laugh like that. And I've got a book as well. (*Takes a book from the bag.*) *Advice on Dying.* I mean, I know it sounds like it might be depressing but it's not. It's actually life-affirming. Not that you're going to die yet. I mean we all die at some point. Even me. I'll die one day. Not before you obviously. I hope not, anyway. For your sake. Well, that would be worse, wouldn't it. I mean, the natural order is best. Your kids dying first, that's unbearable. Anyway, it's about preparation for death. I wasn't going to get it, no one talks about death, do they, not in the West, but Susan said I should give you the option. Just so it's not a taboo. So, you know, if you do want to talk about death, I'm all ears.

Harry Another time maybe.

Frank Fine. I'll leave it anyway. put it there. It's up to you. But just listen to this. (*Puts the CD on.*) I'll light the candle so you get the aroma as well.

Lights the candle. Tibetan monks begin to chant. They listen.

Susan wants this on her deathbed. (*Pause.*) Not that I'm saying – Dad, I mean you don't have to be dying to listen to this. I mean, you know, I listen to it. I love it. And you're not dying anyway. You won't die. Not yet. We'll beat this. Drink that juice.

Harry If I do die . . .

Pause. Frank turns the music down.

Frank Yeah?

Harry If I do die. I'd rather go out to Satchmo, thanks.

Frank Oh. Yeah, well, of course. Sorry, Dad. Okay. Well, come the time I'll do it, I'll be there, promise. You'll go out to Louis Armstrong. What I'll actually do is, I'll put him on the moment we think you're actually dead. Because, apparently, after that your brain can still hear. The last thing to go is your hearing. So I'll put him on then.

Harry Put him on before that.

Frank Oh, yeah, alright. Whatever you want. I'll do it. When the time comes. So 2050, then.

The front door opens and closes. Terry enters.

Terry Oh fuck me. It stinks. Am I in a fuckin' brothel?

Harry I like it.

Terry And who's that? (*Listens for a beat.*) That's Dizzee Rascal, isn't it? (*Laughs.*) Givin' you a bit of aromatherapy, is he, Dad? Poof.

Harry Leave him alone.

Terry Just showin' an interest in his job.

Frank How's the mini-cabbing?

Terry Shite. Now what's so urgent? I've got a pick-up in ten minutes.

Harry It's about the house.

Terry The house?

Harry This house.

Frank What about it?

Harry I wanna buy it. I've looked into it. I've still got the right to buy. I'm still due forty per cent off.

Terry Fuckin' 'ell. Twenty years ago I told him to buy it. 'No, no. It's wrong.'

Harry It is wrong.

Terry Thirty thousand he could've bought it for. Thatcher started givin' 'em away. 'I don't want nothin' off that witch.'

Harry I don't want nothing off that witch. I feel like she's won.

Frank If you don't want to do it, Dad, don't do it.

Harry Soon I'll be gone, and this is the only thing of value I can pass on.

Frank Dad, you are leaving us a lot more than money.

Terry Yeah but, you know, that's alright but, well, it'd be nice to have some money as well, won't it.

Harry I've had an estate agent round.

Terry That's all we need.

Harry He reckons it's worth two hundred thousand.

Terry It's worth more than that. Jack Reed's place went for two-twenty. Dolly Dawson bought it last year. We'll get a second opinion. Bung a dodgy agent a few quid to bump it up.

Frank We want to bump it down, not up. We're buyin' it, you mong.

Harry So we can buy it for a hundred and twenty.

Terry Hundred and twenty? Gotta do that.

Harry I want to make sure the grandchildren are looked after. The problem's the mortgage. I can't get one.

Terry I'll get one for you. I know someone who can get any idiot a mortgage. He got me one. Actually, he's got me five mortgages. I first bought it for fifty. He's helped me get four re-mortgages, I owe a hundred and sixty on it now. It's only worth a hundred and forty.

Frank I'll get Suze on the case.

Harry Are you sure? I didn't want to bother her.

Frank Dad, she's an estate agent. I don't know why you didn't ask.

Harry I know how busy she is.

Frank Dad, you know she'd do anything for you.

Terry And there's a few quid in it for her.

Frank She won't charge a penny, if that's what you're implying.

Terry Imply? Me? I don't know what it means.

Frank Don't you worry about a thing, Dad. Suze'll take care of everything.

Terry She'd better get on to it quick, like. We don't know how long we've got.

Frank There's plenty of time.

Harry I'm not goin' anywhere yet.

Frank Soon as I get home I'll get her on to it. I'd better go. Gotta pick up the bairns.

Terry Woman.

Frank I'll bring 'em over at the weekend.

Harry That'd be lovely.

Frank hugs Harry. He holds on. Harry taps Frank's back, signalling him to let go. Frank lets go.

Frank Drink that juice.

Frank exits.

Terry Bender.

Harry Well, off you go then, you've got a pick-up.

Terry I'm nearly out of petrol. I've been doin' a lot of account work. I'll be flush on Friday, and I'll have cash jobs later.

Harry How much?

Terry Fifty to fill up now.

Harry Fifty?

Terry My life. Hardly worth doin' this job.

Harry (*looks in his wallet*) Oil companies. Robbers. Thieves. I've not got fifty. Twenty.

Terry That'll do. You'll have it Friday. Cross my heart.

Harry I can't afford to pay the bills, let alone lose money to you.

He gives Terry a twenty.

Terry Cheers, Dad. Sorry. Friday. On me life. (*Exits.*)

Harry I don't get it, Gracie. Do you? We've got brains, haven't we? How did we breed a couple of bloody idiots?

He sits in his armchair. Switches on the CD player, Charlie Parker, 'Now is the Time'. Lights fade to black.

SCENE THREE

Lorraine, mid-forties, sits on the sofa, nervously playing with a packet of cigarettes. Terry sits in Harry's armchair reading the Daily Mirror *sports pages. Harry, wearing a cap to cover hair loss, pops his head through the hatch.*

Harry How many sugars?

Terry You know how many sugars.

Los Three, please.

Terry How many times has he made you a cup of tea?

Los His memory's goin'.

Terry He's getting' that thing, isn't he?

Los What thing?

Terry That thing, you know, where you forget things. What's it called?

Harry Alzheimer's?

Terry That's right. You're gettin' Alzheimer's.

Harry What?

Terry You're gettin' Alzheimer's.

Harry What?

Terry Oh, shut up.

Harry Who are you? Who's that, Los? Who is he?

Los He's a fuckin' twat.

Harry Oh yeah, that's it. I remember him now.

Terry He is though, he's gettin' that Alz thing.

Los That's the radiotherapy, that is. My Uncle Arthur lost loads of brain cells when he started that. Everyone does.

Harry enters with a mug of tea.

Harry How many sugars?

Terry You know what you're gonna need soon, don't you. A carer.

Harry I'm alright.

Terry Not soon, you won't be.

Harry I can look after myself.

Terry It takes months to organise. We should get on to it now.

Los He's right, Harry. They string it out, the Nash. They're hopin' you die before they have to splash the cash. You ask anyone who's applied for it.

Terry Los'll do it.

Los I wouldn't mind.

Terry Might as well let us have the money instead of a stranger.

25

Los I'd do it anyway. That's not why I'd do it. But if money's goin', I might as well have it.

Terry And if you work it, when they come round, play it up, pretend you're worse than you are.

Los Say your mind's gone.

Terry You wouldn't be fuckin' lyin' about that.

Los Say you're confused about your pills. You can't feed yourself. You need someone to help you get dressed.

Terry Say you need someone in the mornin', the middle of the day, early evening, and last thing at night.

Harry I don't want anyone in here four times a day. I wanna be free to go out whenever I want. I don't want anyone doing anything for me.

Terry That's what we mean. That's why Los is the best person for it. She won't do fuckin' owt, her.

Los I won't. I won't lift a finger, promise. I'll just phone you up. If you're alright I'll leave you alone. If you need me, I'll pop round. Or I'll send one of the kids.

Harry I don't need it.

Terry But you will. Look in the mirror. It's not fuckin' good.

Los Any biscuits?

Harry I'll just get 'em.

Terry I'll get the forms, anyway. We'll have 'em ready.

The doorbell rings and a key turns in the front door.

Here they are, the apron and his boss. (*Laughs.*)

Frank enters carrying a full M&S carrier bag and a bag from an off-licence. Susan, mid-forties, wearing a suit, follows him in.

Susan Hi.

Los Hello.

Terry Hello.

Susan Harry. (*Hugs him.*)

Harry Hello, pet.

Susan Aah.

Frank You alright, Dad? (*Hugs him.*)

Harry Fine.

Susan Fine? You look great. He looks great, doesn't he, darling?

Terry He don't.

Frank You look fantastic. That's the alfalfa, that is.

Terry Are you blind?

Susan You're going to beat this, Harry.

Terry Not without a carer, he won't.

Susan We've bought some fruit for you. Where's the fruit, darling?

Frank There you go.

Frank gives Susan the M&S carrier bag.

Susan Harry, I want you to promise me that you'll eat this fruit.

Harry I love a bit of fruit.

Frank Blueberries, Dad.

Susan Blueberries, Harry. Blueberries, blueberries, and more blueberries.

Frank They're a superfood.

Susan Full of anti-oxidants.

Frank To fight cancer.

Harry Who wants tea?

Susan Don't you dare. You sit down. Don't you move. You shouldn't be doing anything. Frank, darling, make the tea.

Terry Mine's a coffee.

Los I've just got one. Can you bring the biscuits in?

Harry Tea for me.

Frank Darling?

Susan Not for me, darling. Just pop that thing in the freezer for five minutes. We've brought something to celebrate with, Harry.

Terry Is it sorted?

Susan It can be, Terry. It can be and it will be.

Terry Forget my coffee, slave. I'll have some of that thing too.

Los Well, if we're celebrating . . .

Susan We are celebrating.

Frank exits to the kitchen.

Harry We've got it then?

Susan We have. It's not been easy because of your age and health, Harry. The best way round, to get the best deal, is for us to be your guarantor. So we have to put our house up as security.

Harry No, no. You can't do that.

Susan We want to.

Harry Let's just forget it. I don't want to put your house under threat. You've got the bairns to think about.

Susan That's exactly who we are thinking about. When we eventually sell this, Harry, it'll pay the school fees. It makes sense. There's no threat to our house. We've got huge equity. You've got huge equity because of the discount.

Frank pops his head through the hatch.

Frank We did it last year with a 'buy to let'. (*His head disappears back into the kitchen.*)

Terry You've got a 'buy to let'?

Susan We've got several.

Terry Several?

Frank (*pops his head in again*) It's a golden goose. (*Head disappears.*)

Susan The rent we get more than pays the mortgage.

Frank (*pops his head in again*) It's our pension. (*Head disappears.*)

Harry No. I've changed my mind.

Susan Harry, trust me. I'm an estate agent. I know what I'm talking about.

Terry Yeah, she knows. Don't argue with a fuckin' expert.

Susan And the other thing we want to do is, we want to borrow some extra money so that you can have a dream holiday.

Harry I don't want a dream holiday.

Susan The thing is, because of the equity, they're willing to give us as much money as we want.

Frank (*head in*) They actually want to give us a hundred and twenty per cent of what this house is actually worth. (*Head disappears.*)

Susan It's sound business, actually. So what we want to do is borrow a few thousand pounds extra for you, so that you can do whatever you want before it's too late.

Harry No, no, no . . .

Susan It's your money, Harry. Spend it.

Frank (*head in*) Where d'you wanna go, Dad? The world's your oyster. (*Head out.*)

Harry I don't feel up to goin' anywhere.

Susan Well, you might change your mind when you start to feel better.

Terry He's not gonna feel any fuckin' better. And he doesn't want to die abroad. He wants to die at home.

Frank (*head in*) Well, he can have the money, anyway. Just to make life easier. Give him a bit of luxury.

Harry I would like to pay off my credit card.

Frank Well, there you go, you can pay off your debts, and do whatever you want with the rest. (*Head out.*)

Susan And we're happy to pay the extra on the mortgage for you.

Terry We can't. We can't afford our own fuckin' mortgage.

Frank (*head in*) We're talkin' about us. We know you can't. (*Out.*)

Susan Because actually, what we want to do –

Frank (*in*) Because it's such a great rate we're getting. (*Out.*)

Susan We'd like to release Frank's half of the inheritance, so that we can use it now.

Terry What's that?

Susan Well, the thing is, we were thinking of using the collateral on our house to borrow forty so that we could turn the loft into a holistic haven for Frank's aromatherapy. But if we use it to help buy this, the only way we can do the loft is by releasing what will be his soon anyway, through the extra on the mortgage.

Frank Champagne, anyone?

Through the hatch comes a tray with five glasses of champagne and a well-presented bowl of garnished strawberries with a pot of cream.

Terry (*jumps up*) Oh, look at this, Nigella's been at it. Fuckin' 'ell. (*Takes the tray.*) Show us your tits.

Los Hold on. If Frank's getting his half now, it's only fair Terry gets the same.

Terry Actually, yeah, that's true. And we're goin' down the fuckin' tubes, we are.

Los We've had the bailiffs round.

Terry We're gonna lose our house if we don't stump up six in a few weeks.

Los Six? You said three.

Terry Yeah. No. Well. I dunno. Six, three, I don't do fuckin' mathematics, do I?

Frank enters.

Frank We've put our house up as collateral.

Terry We'll put our house up.

Frank You don't own a single brick of it.

Terry I'll get a dodgy valuation. We can get dodgy fuckin' equity.

Harry Right. Stop this now. I'm not going through with it.

Frank I told you he'd mess it up.

Terry You're fuckin' it up. Not me.

Harry I wish I'd never brought it up.

Susan Hold on. Hold on, everyone. Let's just calm down. It's fine. It's absolutely fine. If Terry wants his now I don't see why he can't have it.

Terry Really?

Los We can have it?

Susan You can have it.

Harry I don't like this. It's not right.

Terry Not right? You're saving our fuckin' lives. You're keeping a roof over wor bairns' heads. How can that be not fucking right?

Los (*in tears*) Thanks, Harry. Thank you. (*Hugs him.*) And thank you, Sue. That's such a relief. Thank you.

   Susan and Los hug.

Susan Aah. I'm just glad we can help.

Terry Party!

Los Let's get mortal.

Terry Eh, Dad, you're gonna be a capitalist bastard.

Los You'll be votin' Tory next.

Terry Maggie, Maggie, Maggie. In, in, in.

Harry Don't you dare. I'm not happy about it as it is. I can always change my mind.

Los If she was here now, I'd kiss her fuckin' arse.

Harry No one kisses that woman's arse in my house! There's a line. I might've moved it. But there's still a line. And Thatcher's arse is it.

They laugh.

Terry Holiday. We can have a fuckin' holiday.

Los The Maldives. I've always wanted to go to the Maldives.

Frank We did the Maldives, last Christmas.

Susan Well, we wanted to go before it sank.

Harry Sank?

Terry Is it sinkin'?

Frank Global warming, Dad. That's one thing you won't miss.

Susan We said to ourselves, there's two things we want to see before it's too late. The Maldives before it goes under . . .

Frank And Greenland before it melts.

Susan But the children don't want to go to Greenland at the moment.

Frank They don't have kids' clubs.

Susan What can you do? We're raising a generation of entertainment junkies.

Frank So we'll probably bite the bullet and do Mauritius instead.

Susan This year, anyway.

Terry So, Sue, our mortgage. Who's it with?

Susan Northern Rock.

Terry Howay the lads. I'll drink to that. (*Raises his glass.*) Northern Rock.

They all toast.

All Northern Rock.

Blackout.

SCENE FOUR

Eight months later. Terry sits at the table chopping a line of coke, smoking a spliff and watching Sky Sports News. A key turns in the front door, he looks over as it opens and puts his hand over the coke to hide it as Susan steps in with a full Sainsbury's shopping bag.

Susan Oh. Hi.

Susan closes the door behind her.

Terry What you doin' here?

Susan I wanted to put out some flowers and stock the fridge for when they get back.

Terry Sorry I couldn't pick 'em up. I'm working. (*Tokes.*)

Susan Looks like it.

She takes a potted plant from the carrier bag.

Terry Not my fault there's no jobs. I've still gotta be on call.

Susan They've had to get an airport taxi.

Terry Have they had a good time? (*Laughs.*)

Susan As a matter of fact they've had a wonderful time. They've really bonded.

Terry Of all the places. Where d'you wanna go in the world, Dad? What's your dream holiday? Frank puts his hand up, I'll come with you, Dad. I bet he was thinking Disneyland, the Pyramids, New York. No. Dunkirk. (*Tokes.*)

Susan If you must smoke that at least open a window.

Terry Dunkirk. (*Laughs.*)

Terry gets up from the chair and opens a window. Susan sees the coke.

Terry Oh that, yeah. It's er . . .

Susan I know what it is.

Terry Yeah, well, I'm a . . .

Susan Waste of space?

Terry Addict.

Susan Really? Are you really an addict?

Terry Yeah. A sex addict. D'you want some?

Susan Excuse me?

Terry Coke. D'you want a line?

Susan No, thank you.

Terry wipes the coke up with a finger, rubs it into his gums and pockets the wrap. Susan places the plant on a window sill.

Terry Or the other?

Susan What?

Terry Sex. D'you want some?

Susan Fuck off.

Terry I'm good at it. I've got a good one. Bigger than Frank's.

Susan How dare you?

Terry Nightmare, this credit crunch thing, isn't it? People aren't goin' out. No one's gettin' taxis. You lot are in the shite, aren't you? Estate agents.

Susan No. It's not as bad as it's being painted, actually. We're okay. It'll sort itself out. It's being overdone in the media. We've seen it all before in the eighties. Okay, so the glory days have gone. But they'll be back. It's just tighten your belt time. The love affair with property is just on hold. The end is not nigh.

A taxi pulls up outside. Susan looks out.

Susan There they are.

Terry Saved by the bell.

Terry extinguishes the spliff. Susan opens the front door and waves.

Susan Hello, darling.

Frank enters and they hug and kiss.

Missed you.

Frank Me too. Love you.

Terry Dunkirk. (*Laughs as he exits.*)

Frank You got twenty? I'm short for the taxi. The cashpoint wouldn't give me anything. It's a mistake, isn't it?

Susan We'll talk later. It's fine.

She gives Frank her purse.

Frank It is a mistake, isn't it?

Susan Just pay him. Everything's fine.

Harry, wearing an NHS wig, enters with a duty-free bag. Frank exits.

Harry. Aah.

Harry Hello, pet.

They hug.

Susan Did you have a good time?

Terry enters with two suitcases.

Harry I had a wonderful time. I can honestly say it's been the best week I've had since I can't remember.

Terry You can't remember. That's the fuckin' thing, isn't it? You might've had a better time a few weeks ago, but you wouldn't fuckin' remember it if you had.

Susan Take your dad's cases up to his bedroom.

Terry What did your last slave die of?

Susan And unpack them.

Terry I'm not a woman. (*Exit.*)

Susan Tea?

Harry Champagne. (*Holds up his duty-free bag.*)

Susan You devil.

She takes Harry's coat and the champagne.

You sit.

Harry I will if you don't mind.

Frank enters.

Susan I'm so glad you had the time together.

Frank It was great.

Frank puts his arm around his dad's shoulder. Harry reciprocates.

Harry It was wonderful, son.

Susan Honours, darling.

He gives Frank the champagne.

Frank I told him not to waste his money. He insisted.

Susan If Harry wants 'ampagne, he should have 'ampagne.

Frank exits to the kitchen.

Harry I got the urge to go and see where my dad died.

Susan I know, Harry, that's why you went.

Harry I didn't know him, see.

Susan I know, Harry.

Harry There was a whole generation of us who never knew our dads. And then a lot of 'em who did come back weren't fit for much.

Susan I know, Harry.

Harry Kids today haven't got a clue.

Susan I know, Harry.

Harry My mum used to get up at half past four every mornin' and queue up for cracked eggs so that we'd have breakfast.

Susan I know, Harry. We don't know we're born, my generation. And as for our children . . .

Harry How are they? Are they alright?

Susan Fine. They're lovely. Busy though. I'll bring them over soon. I promise.

Harry That'd be nice.

Susan It's these bloody clubs. Tae Kwon Do, Saturday morning. Swimming, Saturday afternoons. Football Sunday mornings. And then weekdays, after-school clubs in Piano, Hockey, and Mandarin.

Harry Mandarin?

Susan It's the future, Harry. They have to be prepared.

Harry They're kids, pet. Not chickens.

Susan What?

Harry Nothin', pet, sorry. I just, you know . . . Don't you worry about it. You're doin' a good job.

Terry enters.

Terry Alright. I'm off.

Los (*off*) Cooeee.

Terry Oh no, fuck.

Los enters, sees Terry.

Los What the fuck are you doin' here?

Terry What? Oh . . .

Los Half an hour ago you phoned me from fuckin' Manchester. You got a private fuckin' jet, have you?

Terry No. No fuck. No. No. I was on me way back. I'd been.

Los You've been?

Terry Yeah, yeah, no fuckin' traffic. Unreal. Straight through. And back. Unfuckinbelievable.

Los Aye. It fuckin' is.

Terry Anyway, I'm off, I've got another fuckin' pick-up.

Harry Not yet you're not. I've got some news. That's why I wanted everyone here.

Frank enters with the poured champagne.

Frank Is that what this is about?

Harry It is, son. Get your glasses, everyone.

The champagne is handed round.

Los Tell me you've won the fuckin' lottery, man.

Harry Better than that. Much, much better.

Terry Dennis Wise is dead. Gan on, man. Tell me fuckin' Dennis Wise is dead.

Harry It's the most amazing thing.

Frank What, Dad?

Harry Yesterday evening I had a phone call from the consultant, when you were in the bar.

Frank Why didn't you tell me?

Harry I wasn't sure I didn't imagine it until I checked it with him again this morning. I kept thinkin' it might have been a dream. But it's true.

Terry What?

Harry Well, it's the most wonderful news. I'm in the clear. The cancer's gone. The chemotherapy worked. They don't want to see me for three months. And he's confident. He says to me it's gone. Not a trace. He reckons I could live to a hundred.

Pause.

Los You fuckin' beauty. (*Gives Harry a big hug.*)

Susan Harry, that's the most marvelous news I've ever heard. (*Hugs him.*)

Frank I love you, dad. (*Hugs him.*)

Susan I knew you'd beat it.

Terry I don't believe it. You sure?

Los Of course he's fuckin' sure.

Terry I'm just sayin'. His brain's gone, hasn't it?

Los His brain's gone? Shut up, you twat. It's better news than Kevin fuckin' Keegan, man. Now give your dad a fuckin' hug.

Terry Yeah, yeah, great fuckin' news, dad. Great. (*He gives Harry a quick, awkward hug.*) Well done. Well fuckin' done.

Susan raises her glass.

Susan Harry.

Terry I'll drink to that.

They toast.

All Harry.

They drink.

Terry You know what, though, you know fuckin' what. We should sue. The NHS, we should sue their fuckin' arses.

Harry What?

Terry I bet you could get thirty thousand out of this.

Los Aye man, that's right. That's what Jerry Harris wangled.

Terry They told him he had indigestion.

Los It was a heart attack. Thirty grand in his back pocket.

Terry I'd have a heart attack for thirty grand.

Los If you were insured, I'd fuckin' arrange one.

Harry They've just saved my life.

Terry Yeah, but look at the stress they've caused you.

Los And us. We've been through it too.

Terry They virtually told us you were a goner.

Harry I'm gonna live, son. I'm gonna live. I love you, Terry. I love you. And you, Frank. I love you too. I love you so much. I love my boys. I love 'em. And their girls. I love my family. And I'm so happy I'm gonna be around to see 'em a bit longer. And I want to appreciate things more. Do things. You only live once. This is it. I know I'm old, but there are things I would really like to do. See things I've never seen. Go places I've never been. Have we got any more equity left we can cash in on our mortgage?

Blackout.

SCENE FIVE

A year later. Terry smokes a spliff and watches News 24.
The markets are crashing across the globe. The front
door opens and Frank enters carrying a full Morrison's
shopping bag.

Frank Where's Dad?

Terry Gone doggin'. (*Beat.*) I dunno, do I? Am I his
keeper?

Frank You haven't paid your part of his mortgage this
month.

Terry I'll catch up next month.

Frank Oh yeah.

Terry Alright, I won't.

Frank If we fall too far behind they could repossess this
place.

Terry It's the end of capitalism. What's the point in payin'
a mortgage? We'll have a revolution soon.

Frank I've had to take a job as a chauffeur.

Terry A chauffeur? Mini-cabbin', you mean?

Frank A suit. You have to wear a suit. And they provide
the cars. It's an upmarket clientele.

Terry They're the worst. Treat you like a servant, don't
they?

Frank I won't be doing it for ever. I'm going to retrain.

Terry I've been offered another job. Twice the money,
too.

Frank Yeah?

43

Terry Debt collector.

Frank Oh, well, you know, if it's twice the money.

Terry I've got principles. I'm not a knuckleduster.

Frank We're in the shit. You need to find the money for this mortgage. We could lose everythin'.

Terry Join the club.

Frank Oh fuck it. Gimme that spliff. I need to calm down.

Terry hands Frank the spliff.

Frank I feel like I'm having a heart attack. I've got palpitations. (*Tokes on the spliff.*) We have to get real here.

Terry D'you want some coke?

Frank What?

Terry I've got a bit of coke. D'you want a line?

Frank You haven't paid the mortgage.

Terry I know. But, you know, you gotta live a bit, haven't you?

Frank I give up.

Terry So do I. That's why, you know, you might as well. We're all goin' down the tubes. Look at the telly. Everyone's jumpin' into my boat now. Let's have a fuckin' sinkin' party.

Frank Look, the thing is, er . . . (*Tokes.*)

Terry Oi. Bogart.

Frank Sorry. (*Hands spliff back.*) Nice.

Terry Does the trick.

Frank The thing is er . . . oh, shit. Oh, no. Oh, God.

Frank goes down on to his hands and knees. Terry laughs. Frank groans and lies flat on the floor.

Terry You still can't take drugs, you fuckin' lezzer. (*Laughs.*)

Frank moans. Terry laughs more.

Blood, that's what you need. Blood to your head. I'll kick your fuckin' head in, shall I? (*Laughs.*) Howay, knees up.

Terry helps Frank turn over and put his knees up. Frank groans. Terry jumps on Frank between his legs and pretends to shag him.

Baby, I love you, baby.

Frank Fuck off!

Terry Howay, you bitch. You know you fuckin' love it.

Frank Get off.

Terry shags like a jackhammer.

Terry You're beautiful. You're so fuckin' beautiful.

Frank begins to laugh.

Oh, you're enjoying it now, aren't you? You're fuckin' loving it. Squeal, piggy. Fuckin' squeal.

Frank (*laughing*) Stop. Stop.

Terry (*pretends to come*) Ooohhhhh!

They both crack up laughing, and Terry rolls off Frank. The laughter subsides and becomes a pause.

Frank Good gear, that.

Terry I know.

Frank Strong.

Terry I know.

Frank I'd forgotten how nice drugs can be.

Terry You should try Prozac. Alright, it is.

Frank Are you on Prozac?

Terry You know what. This is true. I'll tell you what. No matter how shite everythin' looks. No matter like if it's all goin' down the drain. You can be like, you know, well we got the bailiffs comin' round, yeah, so I'm like, aye, it's a nightmare, aye, we might not have anywhere to live, but you know, I feel not too bad about it. Prozac that is.

Frank Get the coke out. Go on. Sod it. I need to get wrecked.

Terry Yes! For ever young! (*Takes a wrap from his pocket.*) He's still got champagne from his live-for-ever party in the fridge. Get it, slave. I'll replace it.

Frank This is the life I should be living. Oh God, I wish I was a student again. (*Exits.*)

Terry chops up a couple of lines.

Terry Thing is, yeah, I was thinking, you know, everyone's worried about where to put their money, with the stock market and all that. I know where to put it. I know.

Frank comes in with a bottle of champagne and two glasses.

Frank Where?

Terry Anti-depressants. I'm telling' you this, there's one thing that's definitely gonna go up – downers.

Frank D'you know what, that's brilliant. If we had money, that's where we should put it.

46

Terry Couldn't we borrow some?

Frank I think we've all borrowed enough. I think that's the point. It's time to start payin' it back.

Frank pops the cork and pours two glasses of champagne.

Only one answer I can see. Let's get smashed.

Terry Geronimo. (*Snorts a line.*)

Frank Bottoms up.

Terry In one.

They both down their champagne in one.

Geronimo! (*Points at the line.*)

Frank Geronimo! (*Snorts the line.*)

Terry One more for luck?

Frank Go for it.

Terry chops two more lines. Frank pours more champagne.

Terry Funeral directors. That's a job that's gonna do well out of this. People dying of worry, jumpin' off bridges. That's something you might want to look into.

Frank No. I'll be one of them jumping.

Terry The police. Crimes gonna fuckin' go through the roof. What about one of those, you know, pretend policemen, community fuckin' service plods. I can see you as one of them.

Frank There's a few people out there I'd love to lock up. You could be my first arrest.

Terry Marriage counsellors. They're gonna do alright out of this too.

Frank That's another great idea. You know what? You're not as thick as everyone thinks you are. I can see myself as a marriage counsellor. (*Snorts a line.*)

Terry You'd need one if she saw you now.

Frank You're joking. She loves Charlie. Well, not since we've got kids. But if she was here now she'd join us. She'd love to get smashed. God knows she needs to. She's had to lay everyone off. And that's cost a packet. She's sittin' in her office from eight a.m. to nine p.m. No heating, half the lights off, staring down a barrel. She's sold one house in the last month. And that was – I felt so sorry for the owners – eighty-foot, landscaped south-facing garden, a Zen corner, a beautiful . . . not a shed, a summerhouse, I mean you could live in this thing. To be honest we could end up there. Six bedrooms, double fronted, original features, two master bedrooms. A forty thousand pound loft, this was a flat in itself, its own bathroom, velux windows, if you stick your head out through the roof, panoramic views of Gosforth. Perfect for an au pair.

Terry A Swedish au pair. (*Pretends to masturbate.*) Swedish. If I ever had an au pair I'd want her to be Swedish.

Frank You couldn't afford a Latvian one, let alone a Swedish.

Terry I can dream.

Frank A year ago this house would have been worth four seventy-five. It went for four hundred. Four hundred. Four hundred! It's good coke this.

Terry Just say no. (*Snorts.*)

Frank The point is, though, we've had it. I mean, we might well go bankrupt. It's the buy-to-lets, they've done us in. We've massively overstretched ourselves. So . . . Look . . . What d'you think of us moving Dad into a smaller place? I mean we've got a fantastic flat for an old person. It's really near us.

Terry No.

Frank This place is too big for him now anyway.

Terry No.

Frank We can't afford to pay the mortgage any more. You can't pay yours . . .

Terry I'll find it.

Frank What, in the betting shop?

Terry Stranger things have happened.

Frank You can't pay. We can't pay.

Terry I'll get my bit.

Frank How?

Terry I'll rob a bank.

Frank It's like talking to a two-year-old. And anyway, if you do rob one, you might find there's no fucking money in it!

Terry This is his house. He's lived here for fifty years.

Frank It won't be his house if we don't pay the mortgage. It'll be the bank's.

Terry You're only worried about yourself.

Frank What?

Terry Well, if he loses this, that means you lose yours. That was the deal, wasn't it?

Frank I hate you, you know that.

Terry I love you.

Frank You hate me.

Terry It's a thin line.

Frank No, it's not.

Terry Alright, it's a thick line. Like me.

Frank You'd love to see me go under, wouldn't you? Even if it means Dad getting thrown on the street.

Terry You're the one who wants to move him, not me.

Frank You are a total and utter moron.

Terry I fuckin' know!

Terry launches himself at Frank and gets him in a headlock. Frank struggles to get free.

Come on then. Come on. Mummy's favourite. Mummy's little boy.

Frank gives up the struggle. Terry starts repeatedly slapping him on the forehead. Frank struggles again.

Bring back memories. Eh? Happy days? First day at school, yeah? Remember this, your first day at school? All the way there.

Sings and continues slapping Frank on the forehead.

Oh me lads, you should've seen us gannin',
Passing the folks along the road
Just as they were stannin'
All the lads and lasses there
All with smilin' faces –

Harry enters wearing a shirt and trousers, but looking dishevelled.

Gannin' along the Scotswood Road,
To see the Blaydon Races.

Terry sees Harry and stops. Pause. He lets Frank go.

He was askin' for it.

Frank It's okay, Dad.

Harry You've always bullied him.

Terry Someone has to. He's got no fuckin' morals. He wants to move you out the house. He wants to sell this place and put you in one of his buy-to-lets.

Harry looks at Frank. Pause.

Frank We're goin' under, Dad. The business is on the floor. Suze is looking to find another job, the buy-to-lets are like a lead weight, and it's all tied into our house, and although in theory there's still equity in some of the flats, there aren't any buyers, so it's meaningless. We can't afford next term's school fees, the kids might have to go to the local state school which is fine but . . . I mean . . . they've been spoilt, so it's gonna be a shock, but that's okay, I think it'll be good for them, I can't stand most of the snotty parents anyway, but the thing is, we could lose the house. We are in fact in serious arrears. And the bank, the bank, last year they couldn't give us enough credit. They were on the phone once a month, 'Would you like a twenty-thousand-pound loan?' Every time I went in they were trying to give me more, or sell me insurance, they wanted to throw in a free car breakdown service. Now, now they're playing hardball and . . . The thing is, Dad . . . This house . . . If we don't sell it we're gonna lose it anyway. And . . . I mean, you know, we wish you could actually come and live with us but it's just not big enough. Although if you wanted to, I could turn the kids' playroom into a bedroom. But look, look, it's fine. Forget it. We'll manage. I don't know how, but we will. Just, you know, if you want to be nearer to us. But forget it. Honestly. What you wearing? Where you been? It's freezing. I hope you haven't been out like that?

Terry You'll catch your death.

Harry Where's my jacket? I had it on.

Terry I told you. He needs a fuckin' carer.

Harry I don't.

Terry He's not eatin' right, either. He needs someone to feed him.

Frank That's one of the reasons I was thinking' about getting' you nearer us, Dad. You've stopped juicing, haven't you?

Terry He don't need juice. He needs a carer.

Frank I brought some alfalfa and carrots with me.

Harry I don't want alfalfa! And I don't want a bloody carer! You've had your inheritance! The cupboard's bare! Leave me alone!

Pause.

Frank We're only thinking of what's best for you.

Terry That's right.

Harry Is that my champagne?

Frank Er, yeah. I'll replace it.

Harry Celebratin', are you?

Terry Yeah. The, er, the demise of capitalism. (*On the TV.*)

Pause.

Harry Well, I'll drink to that.

Frank I'll get you a glass.

He exits and re-enters during the next speech.

Harry (*looking at the TV*) Steal a teabag and they lock you up. Steal fifty million, you get a yacht and a government handout. Con merchants in pin-stripe suits. 'Assets'. That's the con word. 'Assets'. Our debts. This mortgage. To them they're assets. And they're payin' themselves these million-pound bonuses on the basis that we'll pay our debts in the future.

Terry Well, we shouldn't pay 'em then.

Frank You aren't payin' em.

Terry Yeah, well, I'm in the right then, aren't I?

Frank He's not payin' his bit towards your mortgage.

Harry Where's my champagne?

Frank gives Harry his glass. Harry raises it.

The demise of capitalism.

Terry/Frank The demise of capitalism.

They drink.

Harry I knew it was all wrong. Tina Fortune's daughter, she's twenty-one and she's already had three new pairs of breasts.

Terry I know. Wouldn't mind gettin' hold of them.

Harry They look ridiculous. Like a couple of stuck-on rugby balls.

Terry Does it for me.

Harry I saw her in the street a while back, dressed up like a film star, waving her keys to her new BMW. She tells me she's just bought a new three-bedroom house with her boyfriend. I know him. They've not got a brain cell between 'em. He's got a matching BMW. She works as a receptionist, he's a bricklayer. And they thought they owned it all. Debts. That's what they owned. Debts. It was all a mirage. (*Raises his glass.*) Boom and bust.

Terry/Frank Boom and bust.

They drink.

Harry Underneath me and your mam's bed. There's an old brown suitcase. Bring it down.

Terry Why?

Harry To dig us out of a hole, that's why.

Terry What?

Harry There's stuff in there that's worth something.

Terry Like what?

Harry Just get it.

Frank I'll go. (*Exits.*)

Harry What you doin', son?

Terry What?

Harry With your life. What you doin' with it?

Terry Not a lot.

Harry Cut out the ganja.

Terry Ganja? What's that?

Harry The house stinks of it every time you're here.

Terry What, me?

Harry Yeah, you.

Terry No, no, that's er, that's, er, that's my aftershave.

Harry D'you think I'm stupid? D'you think I've never had a joint? How d'you think me and your mum survived when you two were kids? You two? I defy anyone. It was either alcohol, ganja or murder. I wasn't a paragon.

Terry I know that.

Pause.

Harry I know you do. (*Pause.*) All I'm saying is, it's no good for you. It doesn't help in the long run.

Terry I know. That's it. I promise. Honestly. I've stopped. That's it now. I've fuckin' stopped.

Frank enters struggling to lug an old box suitcase.

Frank What's in here? A dead body?

Harry Open it up.

Frank lays the suitcase on the floor by Harry's feet and opens it. They all stare. Pause. Harry tenderly takes an urn from the suitcase.

I forgot it was there.

Pause.

Terry I'll tell you what, I'll never go in a Chapel of Rest again. That was my last image of her, the Chapel of Rest. They'd done her up. Rouge on her cheeks, red lipstick, and they'd pulled the sides of her mouth up. She looked like the fuckin' Joker out of *Batman*. Not Jack Nicholson. The one from the old TV series. Caesar Romero. They reran it on BBC3 last year. I couldn't fuckin' watch it. I kept thinkin' that's Mum in the Chapel of Rest.

Frank My last image of her is looking like an Auschwitz victim. Smiling though. A smiling Auschwitz victim.

Harry I saw her this mornin', lookin' lovely. Just like she used to. She's here most days. It's almost as if I can touch her. It's the house. It's full of memories. Full of life past. Good times. Bad times. The past and the present. It all feels like it's only just happened. It was only a second ago I was a kid. I go down the street and I see all these old faces and I knew them when they were jack the lads or dolly birds. And in my head I'm thinking, they look so old. As if I'm still a young man. And then I'm looking at you two and I'm thinking when did you two get so old. It was only half a second ago when you were born. And me and Mam were . . . The past, see. It's in the walls.

Harry places the urn on the floor and begins taking items from the suitcase.

Harry Family photos. Birth certificates. Death certificate. A cuddly toy.

Frank That's my Teddy.

Terry It's my Teddy.

Frank That's my Teddy. It's only got one eye.

Terry My Teddy only had one eye too.

Frank I know. You pulled them both out. But my Teddy had a left eye missing. Your Teddy had a right eye missing. That is my Teddy.

Terry No. It's mine.

Harry It's my Teddy! I paid for it! It's mine!

Pause. Harry resumes pulling stuff from the suitcase.

Miner's hat. Miner's lamp. A signed photo of Arthur Scargill. That's probably worth something.

Terry What?

Harry As a job lot. The miner's hat, the miner's lamp, and Arthur Scargill.

Terry and Frank laugh.

I'm telling' you. Someone'll want 'em. On eBay.

Frank and Terry crack up laughing.

Terry Is that it? Is that the buried treasure?

Harry Hold on.

Harry looks through the suitcase.

They've gone. Someone's had 'em? Who's had 'em?

Frank Had what?

Harry Your 'unt's diamond necklace she left us. It's been nicked.

Frank You sold it, Dad.

Harry I what?

Terry I told you, he needs help.

Frank You sold it eight years ago for four and a half thousand. Nell, Dad. Auntie Nell. You bought her and the kids over from New Zealand for Uncle Albert's funeral.

Long pause.

Don't worry yourself, Dad. We'll be alright. We'll get the money.

Terry Yeah. I'll get it. I'll get out there now.

Harry I've had enough. I'm ready to go. They keep people alive too long these days. Our bodies are kept goin' but our minds are fallin' apart. We're kept alive by bypasses, five fruit and veg, twenty-five pills, and Sky TV. We're weighin' heavy on the younger generation, we've had our turn. We should be put down. Put me down. I don't want to be a burden.

Frank You're not a burden, Dad.

Terry No, you're a . . . Well, I dunno, but you're not a burden.

57

Harry Alright, I'll go to your flat.

Terry No you fuckin' won't.

Harry I'm going.

Terry I will find the money.

Harry You won't find anything! You waste of fuckin' space! I'll go! (*Pause.*) I'll be fine. I'll go.

Frank The positive thing is, Dad, it's a lovely one-bedroom flat. Fifteen minutes from us in the car. And it's kind of perfect for someone of your age. Ground level, no stairs, living room stroke kitchenette. And I will be round twice a day every day, so will Suze and the boys, you'll be sick of us. We'll take you out. You'll have Sunday lunch with us. We could make it like a holiday. Benwell.

Terry Benwell?

Frank But it's a nice part of Benwell. Up and coming. (*Pause.*) I'm so sorry, Dad.

Harry It's my fault.

Frank No, it's not.

Harry Yes, it is. It was my idea. I bought into it. I knew it was mad. I could see the insanity. But I still caught the gold fever. 'My house is worth a hundred and seventy thousand.' 'Mine's worth two hundred thousand.' 'Mine's worth two hundred and fifty.' Bingo! Two fat ladies! Everyone's a winner! House! House! It's a home! Not just house! A home! (*Pause.*) You know what my dad left me?

Frank I didn't think he left you anything.

Harry He left me loads. And he was born in a North Shields slum.

Frank I know.

Harry You know nowt. When he was not much more than a bairn, his mam, your great-grandmother, died of cholera. Like hundred of others who lived by open sewage. The whole of Low Town had just five toilets and one standpipe for water. Life expectancy was forty-five. And your great-great-granny on your mam's side, she was born in a workhouse. And you know what my dad's dad used to do to earn money to eat when he was ten years old? No state help in those days, you starved if you didn't have money. D'you know what he did?

Frank He shovelled shit.

Harry That's right. He followed police horses round, and when they shat he shovelled it up and knocked on the doors of shipowners in the High Town, selling it for a ha'penny a sack to fertilise home-grown tomatoes. He weren't a fuckin' aromatherapist! No wonder he jumped when Kitchener called. And went over the top at Ypres with the Northumberland Fusiliers for King and Country. Nineteen, he was. Nineteen, when he took a bullet in the head at Passchendaele on the back of a promise of a better life and a 'home fit for heroes'. And I was born in an overcrowded, rat-and-beetle-infested room in Jarrow. In a place they used to call 'consumption row'. Where my dad had crossed the river to escape to, and where he happily broke his back working for Palmer until the crash literally murdered the place. And my mam's brother, your Great Uncle Tommy, walked all the way to London with two hundred others, not to ask for a handout or a freebie, but for work. Work to feed their wives and bairns. They got nowt. Nowt until the war broke out, that is. Then of course, it's your patriotic duty, all of a sudden 'Your Country Needs You' to build ships again. Only my dad was in the Territorials, so he went off with the Durham Lights, and a took a bullet in the back of the head at Dunkirk. And on the back of those men we had a Labour landslide and hundreds of thousands of homes were built. This is one of those homes. This one here. In Low Fell. This, finally, was the 'home fit for a hero'. This was my inheritance. It might not look like much nowadays, but when you realise where it came from. And the cost . . . Sorry, Dad. Sorry.

Pause. Harry gets up and leaves. Fade to black.

SCENE SIX

Five months later. A one-bedroom flat in Benwell, Newcastle. The entire space of living room/kitchenette, bedroom, bathroom, and hall, fits into Harry's old living room. Cardboard boxes full of pictures and other memorabilia are yet to be sorted through. Harry, in boxer shorts and a vest, sleeps restlessly in a new leather armchair. The curtains are closed and the room is lit by News 24 on a giant plasma TV. The door of the flat opens and Susan enters carrying a briefcase. She sees Harry asleep, picks up the remote and turns off the TV. Harry wakes with a start.

Harry What? What?

Susan It's okay, Harry. Only me.

Harry What's this place? Where am I?

Beat.

Susan It's your new flat, Harry.

Harry What?

Beat.

Susan Light, Harry. Let's have some light, see where you are.

She opens the curtains and daylight floods in. Shadows from the security bars fall across the room.

That's better.

Harry The bars! Close the curtains! It feels like a prison!

Pause.

Susan Don't be silly. They're not keeping you in. They're keeping people out. You've got the front door. You're a free man. Oh look, Frank hasn't put the pictures up yet. I'll make sure he does that. A cup of tea, that's what you need.

Harry I'll make it.

Susan I'll make it.

Harry No, no. I've got to get used to everything. I need to practise.

Harry struggles to get up from the chair.

Susan Is the chair not good? I got a recliner for you. Is it not good for getting up?

Harry No, it's fine. I can do it. (*Stands.*) There you go. Good exercise. That's equal to fifty sit-ups at my age. Where are my trousers?

Pause.

Susan The bedroom?

Pause.

Harry Where's that?

Susan I'll have a look.

Harry No, no. I've gotta get the map right in me head. I've got to get it set. (*Looks towards the hallway.*) It's on the right, isn't it?

Susan See, you knew it.

Harry And the bathroom's on the left.

Susan Well done.

Harry I'm really sorry you've had to see me in my underpants.

Susan Don't be silly.

Harry No. There was a time when I wouldn't have minded. When I was a few years younger.

Susan I bet you were a bit of a one, weren't you?

Harry No. I only ever slept with one girl.

Susan Aah. That's so romantic.

Harry I tried it on with twenty or thirty. But she was the only one would have me. She was the only one who said yes.

Susan I bet that's not true.

Harry It is. And I loved her for it. She said yes to me and I fell in love.

Susan I wish I'd have met her. Would she have approved of me?

Harry She's not here.

Susan Sorry?

Harry She stayed at home. She's not here. She's didn't come with us.

Pause.

Susan What d'you mean?

Pause.

Harry Oh, I know. While I think of it. The CD player. I'm really missing my music. I can't work it out.

Susan We've been through this.

Harry I know. But it's all the remotes. I don't know which is which.

Susan Okay. Look.

She demonstrates for what is the fourth or fifth time.

The DVD player is also your CD player.

Harry Got that.

Susan So you switch on the DVD with this remote.

Harry Oh, that one.

Susan Yes, look. Frank's written on it, DVD. So your CDs go in here. Just like a DVD.

Harry Got that.

Susan And this remote's just for TV.

Harry Oh, that one.

Susan Yes. Look Frank's written on it. TV.

Harry Oh yeah.

Susan Red button. On and off.

Harry I don't want the TV. I want the CD.

Susan I know. But the CD plays through the DVD player and you hear it through the TV.

Harry What d'you mean?

Susan Well the music is played through the speakers in the TV so it has to be on.

Harry That's what's confused me. I did that, I get the news.

Susan You have to be on AV1.

Harry What?

Susan This button. This button. Look, we'll work it out. I'll get Frank to go through it with you again. But I'm pushed right now. I've got to meet a client at a property in fifteen and I need you to sign these so we can send them off. Is that okay? I'm sorry. I'm just pushed.

Harry That's okay. I'll wait.

Susan Sorry. Sorry. (*She opens her briefcase.*)

Harry What am I signing?

Susan Housing benefit, and carer's allowance.

> *She gives Harry a pen, puts the documents in front of him and points to where he should sign.*

Susan There, and there.

Harry What's this? Frank's my carer?

Susan That's right.

Harry But what about Anya? She does it all.

Susan Oh, I know but . . . Well she doesn't do it all. Frank's been in most days as well. And anyway, she works for us. We put it in her job description.

Harry Only I don't want to exploit her.

Susan Harry, honestly, she's from Latvia. The money we pay her would buy a castle over there.

Harry But she's not living there, is she? She's living here.

Susan Look, Harry. She's happy. Ask her? Is she happy? Just ask her. If she's not . . . And anyway, look, I mean, I'm trying my best, Harry. I'm trying my best. We are still hanging on by our fingertips. I'm so sorry that you have to live here. I'm so sorry that we had to sell your house. I want to have a nervous breakdown. I do. I want to crack up so that they have to put me away and look after me somewhere with white walls. Somewhere calm. I want to run away. This mad way of living. And the incessant pressure to keep going. To keep things together. To pay the bills. Have the holidays. The school fees. I don't want it. I think it's all wrong. I don't know what I'm doing to my children. They've got transatlantic accents! Fourteen thousand pounds a year on school fees and they've got transatlantic accents! They say 'cool' and 'dude' and 'nigger' and 'bitch'. Sky TV! Sky TV! I told Frank not to get Sky! First it was the Disney Channel. Now it's MTV. I can't control it. I can't control them. They're turning into monsters. Is it me? Am I Frankenstein? I'm useless. It's all wrong. Mary Shelley. If only. 50 cent! Not Mary Shelley! 50 cent and Snoop Doggy Dog! It's wrong! Nothing's right! I hate myself! I don't like who I've become! I can't stand the values that I'm upholding. But I can't stop. I can't crack. If I crack up we lose everything. Everything. I know it's just material wealth. I know we should be happy with less. But I can't face it. I can't face losing it. I don't know who I'll be without it. I don't know who I am with it. I don't know what the point is. What's the point of anything? Why are we here? What are we doing? I don't know. What's the point?

Harry I'll sign! I'll sign! Alright, I'll sign!

*Pause. Susan points out where Harry needs to sign.
Harry signs one of the documents.*

Susan Sorry.

Harry Frank's comin' later then?

Susan No. Not this evening. Anya. Anya's coming to make your tea. Frank's having a back wax.

Harry A what?

Susan It's a modern thing. For modern men.

Harry What is?

Susan He's having the hair removed from his back.

Harry Oh.

Susan He really likes it. We both do. It's a joint decision. He's got to be allowed one little treat, Harry. He's been under such a lot of stress. He loves it. It's like a meditation for him. He says it equals a flotation tank. And he comes back feeling so much better. He'll be here in the morning. And he'll be energised. Like a whirlwind. He'll put all your photos up.

Harry I can do that. I was just asking. You've got your own lives. Don't worry about me. I'm fine.

The intercom buzzes.

What's that?

Susan The intercom.

Harry Intercom?

Susan Frank showed you. (*She picks up the intercom.*) Hello . . . Oh, come in. (*She buzzes the outside door open.*) This button, Harry. Press this and the front door opens.

Harry Who is it?

Susan The Munsters.

Harry Who?

Susan Your other son and his wife.

Harry What do they want?

Susan (*checking the benefit forms*) I don't know. Good question, though. And about time they came over. Oh, Harry, you haven't signed the carer's form.

Harry Oh, sorry.

Susan puts the form in front of him again as Terry enters followed by Los.

Terry Fuckin' 'ell, what's this? A rabbit hutch?

Los Where's your trousers?

Terry Oh my God. Close your eyes, Los. Close your eyes.

Los Where are your trousers, Harry?

Susan In the bedroom.

Los I'll get them. (*Exits.*)

Terry This area's a dump.

Susan Signature please, Harry. I can't be late.

Terry What's that you're signin'? (*Moving in to look.*)

Harry My carer's form.

Terry A carer's form? Who's your fuckin' carer?

Susan Frank. Frank's his carer.

Los enters with Harry's trousers.

Los Frank's his carer?

Terry Frank couldn't care for his own fuckin' arse.

Susan Frank is a natural carer.

Los If he's a natural carer why doesn't he do it for nothin'?

Terry Yeah, fuckin' 'ell. Eleven pound an hour and I'll be a natural fuckin' carer.

67

Susan No wage, no matter how high, could ever make you naturally care about anything but yourself.

Los Don't you fuckin' talk to him like that. I'm the only one talks to him like that.

Terry Yeah, just cos you've been caught with your hands in the till.

Harry I don't want to be the cause of trouble.

Los It's not you, Harry.

Terry No, it's not you, Dad.

Harry I don't want a carer.

Los See, he doesn't want a carer.

Terry That's right, he doesn't want a fuckin' carer.

Harry I don't need a carer.

Terry Yeah, he doesn't need a carer.

Susan (*screams hysterically and tears up the carer's form*) Aaaaggh! Aaaaggh! I don't want to be his carer! I don't want to care! I care too much! I suffer from empathy! I suffer from too much empathy! I should be diagnosed! I am an empathy sufferer!

Terry You're definitely a something sufferer. Schizo-fucking-phrenia in my book.

Los D'you want a Valium? I've got a spare one in my handbag.

Susan I have to go. I've got a viewing. Fingers crossed. The market's on the move again. It's on the move. Onwards and upwards. The signs are there. Green shoots. We're going to be alright, Harry. Everything's going to be fine. (*She hugs him.*) There's a flower in the meadow. A single solitary flower. Okay, it's a dandelion. But I'm going to sell it. I am going to sell it. (*Exits.*)

Los You know what her problem is, don't you? 'Me, me, me. Me, me, me.' She's a fuckin' 'me, me, me' CD.

Harry She's a lovely girl. She's doin' her best.

Los Oh aye, lovely. I wouldn't stick a fuckin' gerbil in here.

Terry Aye, they're taking the piss. You're comin' to live with us.

Los Aye, when we've got somewhere to live, you're comin'.

Harry What d'you mean, somewhere to live?

Terry Threw the keys at 'em, didn't we? Wasn't worth it.

Los He opened the fuckin' door, didn't he? Fuckin' idiot.

Terry He didn't look like a bailiff.

Los And what the fuck does a bailiff look like?

Terry Not like a bummer. This one looked like a fuckin' bummer. I thought it might be one of Frank's mates.

Harry You've lost your house?

Los I've gone from twenty to forty fags a day. I'm a nervous wreck. I can't stop eating doughnuts.

Harry Where you stayin' then?

Terry Oh don't. Nightmare, Dad.

Los Nightmare for us. Not for you, it's not.

Terry No, I know. Canny for me, like.

Los He's got a sauna.

Terry She's got risin' damp and rats.

Los Kevin Mitchell's put him up.

Terry Sauna, power shower, I don't wanna fuckin' leave.

Los B&B. Me and the kids. Stinks, it does.

Terry But, you know, she's tough, she'll stick it out. I said to her, three bedrooms and a garden, nothin' less.

Harry You don't have to stay in a B&B. You can stay here. I don't mind.

Terry Dad, don't, sorry, but you know, I wouldn't stick a fuckin' Afghani in here.

Los And it's the council, Harry. They'll rehouse us if we stick it out.

Terry And when we're in, you're comin' with.

Harry Well . . . We'll see how we go.

Terry How many bedrooms they got? Why can't you live with them? They've got four bedrooms, a study, a playroom, a fuckin' loft.

Harry I don't wanna live with 'em. I don't wanna live with anyone. And I don't wanna be used as a football for you two to fight over. I'm used to my own company. I'll be alright. What was I doin'? I was doin' something.

Los Your trousers.

Harry What?

Terry Your trousers.

Los Trousers.

She gives Harry his trousers.

Terry He's gone downhill, hasn't he? You've only been here a few weeks and you've aged ten years.

Harry I was making a cup of tea.

Los I'll make it.

Harry No, no, I'll make it.

Terry Dad, we really don't want to see your balls.

Harry What?

Terry I just caught a glimpse of 'em. I don't want my wife subjected to that kind of sight. It's not right. Will you put your fuckin' trousers on?

Harry Oh yeah. Sorry. (*Puts his trousers on.*) How many sugars?

Terry Oh, here we go again.

Los Three.

Harry What am I supposed to be doing?

Terry Oh, I can't stand this. I'm going.

Los He's winding you up.

Harry How many sugars?

Los and Harry laugh.

Terry Well, at least you've still got your sense of humour.

Los He needs it here, don't he?

Terry He needs Eric Morecambe on tap to survive this fuckin' place.

They all laugh.

Harry Just like that.

Los Eric Morecambe, you twat, not Tommy Cooper.

Harry Nice to see you, to see you nice.

They all laugh.

Terry Gotta laugh, haven't you. Otherwise you'll cry.

Harry goes into the kitchen.

I feel like cryin'.

Los You've got a power shower. You're laughin'.

Terry Yeah I know, but, you know . . .

Pause.

Los We got owt left on the Barclaycard?

Terry No.

Los What about the Egg?

Terry Joking, aren't you?

Los The Virgin?

Terry No, I fucked the Virgin too. The Goldfish, that's the one, the Goldfish.

Los You've got a Goldfish card?

Terry Yeah, you know, my emergency card. Activated it, never touched it. Four grand on it.

Los Four grand.

Terry Yeah. I hid it so I wouldn't be tempted.

Los Where? Where is it?

Terry I can't fuckin' remember. That's the thing. I've been lookin' for it. I turned the fuckin' house upside down. It's not there.

Los You fuckin' twat.

Terry I know.

Los It's gone then, isn't it? We can't get back in the house.

Terry I know.

Los Well, why d'you bring it up then?

Terry I don't know, you know, I just, I don't know.

Harry enters.

Harry I've got money. How much d'you need? I don't need it.

Los No, Harry. We're fine.

Harry For the kids. I want to give you some for the kids. Let me give you some for the kids.

Los No, no.

Terry No, no. Well, you know . . .

Harry (*takes wallet from trousers.*) Treat 'em. On me, yeah, Grandad.

Terry Alright. If, if it makes you feel better. They're not eatin' right in that place, are they?

Los No, they're not.

Terry McDonald's. That's what they need. Big Macs.

Harry Take whatever's there. I don't need anything.

He gives Terry the wallet.

Terry I'll give it back next time I come over. I'll bring the kids, yeah. They're all missin' you.

Harry Are they?

Los They're doin' my head in. 'Where's Grandad gone?' 'We wanna see Grandad.'

Harry Are they? (*Chokes up.*)

Pause.

Los Aah.

Harry cries. Los hugs him.

Oh, Harry.

Terry You're coming with us, Dad. Promise.

Harry Go on. It's alright. I'm fine. I'm just . . . I'll be okay.

Terry takes all the cash from Harry's wallet and puts ten pounds back.

Terry I've taken forty, yeah. I'll pay you back. Promise.

Harry When you can, son. No hurry.

Terry I've left you with ten.

Harry Take it. I don't need that.

Los No, Harry. No more, please.

Harry Now what was I doin'?

Terry Oh, fuck me.

Los The tea, Harry.

Harry That's right. How many sugars?

Terry Shut up.

Los Was it in an envelope? The Goldfish card? Was it in an envelope with a Goldfish symbol on it?

Terry Yeah.

Los It's with your underpants.

Terry Is it?

Los It's wrapped inside your Newcastle underpants. The lucky ones. The ones you've not washed since Keegan left.

Terry I've been lookin' for them all fuckin' season. Where are they?

Los I can't fuckin' remember. But I've seen 'em. When I was packin' up the house. They're in a bag. They needed washing, I've put them in a bag. It's in one of the suitcases at Mam's.

Terry Let's go.

Los I'm sure it's there.

Terry We'll see you soon, Dad.

Harry Okay.

Los hugs Harry.

Los I'll get Billy to ring you later.

Harry nods.

Terry Come on.

They leave. The front door bangs shut. Pause. Harry closes the curtains.

SCENE SEVEN

The curtains are closed. Harry sits in the leather chair, an open Dosette pill-organiser and a glass of whisky on the coffee table in front of him. The front door opens and bangs shut.

Frank Only me.

Frank enters wearing a Police Community Officer uniform and carrying a full Lidl carrier bag.

Alright, Dad?

He goes straight into the kitchen to stock the fridge.

Harry I've been waitin' for you.

Frank pops his head back in.

Frank One o'clock. I said one o'clock.

Harry In the afternoon. Not night.

Frank It is the afternoon, Dad.

Harry Is it?

Frank Well, if you opened the curtains, you'd see.

Harry I thought it was middle of the night.

Frank Open the curtains and put some trousers on. You might feel better. (*Goes back into the kitchen.*)

Harry I've been waiting for you, anyway. I wanna talk to you.

Frank Yeah, go on then.

Harry That thing you wanted to talk about.

Frank Me? What's that?

Harry Death.

   Pause. Frank enters. Pause.

Frank Okay. Er . . . what d'you want to say?

Harry It doesn't bother me.

   Pause.

Frank Well, erm . . . Well, that's good. There's nothing to be frightened of, Dad. Because erm . . . well . . . we go on.

Harry Where?

Frank Well, er . . . well, you know, erm . . . well, you know, er . . . I dunno, but er . . . See, you know, er . . . well it all depends on what you believe.

Harry I don't believe in anything. I'm just sayin' I don't mind death. It doesn't bother me either way. What's the difference?

   Pause.

Frank I've got some sardines. D'you want a sardine sandwich?

Harry No.

Frank I'm making one. I'll throw in a red onion and a bit of black pepper, that'll cheer you up.

He goes back into the kitchen. Harry resumes taking pills from the Dosette box and washing them down with whisky.

The thing is, Dad, that thing you were saying about . . . about, erm . . .

He comes in again.

Death. Well, er . . . the thing is . . . erm . . . What you doin'? (*Grabs the Dosette box and looks at it.*) What the fuck you doin'? You're on Wednesday's, it's only Monday!

Harry Is it Monday?

Frank Yes, it's Monday. I came on Saturday. It's now Monday and you're on Wednesday's pills.

Harry I thought it was Wednesday.

Frank Well, what happened to Tuesday then?

Harry And Sunday. Where'd Sunday go?

Frank Are you trying to kill yourself?

Harry No. I just dunno what day it is.

Frank Well, open the fucking curtains then!

Pause. Frank goes back into the kitchen.

Harry Forget the black pepper.

Frank comes in again.

Frank I've already done the black pepper.

Harry Already?

Frank Yeah, so it beds in. I put it on first, so the first thing you taste is the tang, then you bite on through. It release the er . . .

Harry Sardines?

Frank Yeah. Well, erm . . . yeah. But listen, yeah, it's only bread. I'll er . . . I'll get two, er . . . other slices. (*Goes back into the kitchen.*)

Harry You're sure it's Monday?

Frank Yes I'm sure it's Monday!

    Pause.

Harry It's that voice again.

    Pause. Frank pops his head in.

Frank What voice?

Harry Your voice.

Frank Well, of course it's my voice. There's no one else in here, is there?

Harry That's the voice you had when you were a kid. It's making a comeback.

Frank What d'you mean?

Harry It's alright, son. I still love you.

    Pause.

Frank And I love you too, Dad.

Harry I know you do.

    Pause. Frank goes back into the kitchen.

And it's definitely Monday, is it?

Pause. Frank pops his head in again.

Frank (*calmly*) Yes, Dad. It's definitely Monday.

Harry Well I'll be blowed.

Pause. Frank goes back into the kitchen.

You got any mayonnaise?

Frank Er . . . (*Looks in the cupboards.*) No.

Harry Never mind.

Frank Mayonnaise and sardines are not a good mix, Dad.

Harry I love it.

Frank comes in with the sardine sandwich.

Frank D'you want a heart attack? That's all I'm sayin'. Do you want a heart attack?

Harry I don't mind.

Beat.

Frank Really nice red onions these. People say Lidl is cheap, but I'll tell you this, they've got better red onions than Waitrose. And you can't say more than that.

He gives Harry the sardine sandwich. Harry takes a bite.

Harry Where did you learn to be such a good cook?

Frank Delia, Dad. Delia.

Harry I don't believe in Heaven.

Frank No, well, it's, er, well, the traditional Christian idea, it's a childlike concept, isn't it? I mean, you know, a happy place full of good people. Well, there wouldn't be many of us there, would there?

Harry Your mum would've made it. If it does exist, she's there.

Frank And if it does exist, Dad, you'll go there too. You'll be together again.

Harry D'you think you'll get there?

Pause.

Frank Well, er, I don't believe in it, so er . . . no. You have to be a believer, apparently. See me, Dad, I kind of believe in . . . well, you know, life, the whole thing, birth, death, the physical plain while we're here. I believe that, er . . . well, it's like a river, it's all happening now. The beginning of your life, the end of your life, past and future events, it's all happening and we're just experiencing it as moments depending on which part of the river we're in. The mountain spring, or the mouth that opens into the sea. For me, you see, Heaven, Hell, it's all within. And without. It just . . . is. And the Heaven and Hell thing, that's just a reflection of how you are. Of your inner state.

Harry Is that right?

Frank Well, er . . . obviously I don't know if it's right. I don't think there is a right. Or a wrong. I don't er . . . I don't know.

Harry I believe in Hell.

Frank Oh. That's a bit bleak. You don't believe in Heaven but you do believe in Hell. Where's Hell then?

Harry Benwell.

Pause.

Frank You need a holiday. That's what you need, a holiday. So do I. I need a holiday too. You know what, Dad, we can make that happen. I've just got a new credit card, nought per cent for a year. Come on, let's do it. I'll come with. Me and you again, the old team. Come on, here it is. (*Takes the card from his wallet.*) The world's your oyster. I'm on the phone (*Picks up the receiver.*) Let's book it, anywhere you want, name that tune. Where am I taking you?

Harry Switzerland.

Pause. A key turns in the look and the flat door opens.

Los Coo-ee. Only me.

Los enters with a bottle of vodka and a couple of Red Bulls. She breaks into song and dance, singing 'Celebration' by Kool and the Gang.

Harry You've got one?

Los continues singing. She pulls Harry up and dances with him.
Then she grabs Frank and dances with him, now performing the theme tune to The Sweeney. *Frank excuses himself from the dance.*

Los He's not a natural, is he, Harry? 'You're nicked for having no fuckin' rhythm.' (*Laughs.*) What d'you think of that then? We're in. We're in. We're fuckin' in. (*Exits into kitchen.*)

Harry That's marvellous.

Los (*enters with glasses*) You should've seen Billy. What an actor. What a performance. He had the social worker in tears. Talk about Robert fuckin' De Niro. That kid, one day, I know he's my own, but one day that boy will win an Oscar.

She pours herself a very large vodka and mixes in a Red Bull.

He was inside the part, you know, he was the part.

Shakin', cryin' his eyes out, real fuckin' tears, and he's scratching away at his eczema, he's bleedin', like he's crackin' up, as if he can't take it no more, the place we're livin'. Brilliant. And I painted Terry really black. I felt terrible. I made him sound a lot worse than he is, and that wasn't fuckin' easy, I tell you.

Harry What d'you say?

Los Oh, you know, he's done a runner, he pays nothin' towards the kids, he does drugs, and worse, much worse. I didn't fuckin' recognise him. Well that's not true, I did, but you know. Points, see. Points, Harry. It's all about housing points. Come on, Frank, a celebratory drink.

Frank I'm on duty. I have to go.

Los Well, nick a fuckin' Mackem for me, man. You'll have one with me, won't you, Harry?

Harry Aye please.

Frank Dad, that is a lethal mix.

Harry I know. That's what I want. Make it a large one, Los.

Los That's my boy.

She pours Harry a large one of the same.

Frank I'm off then.

Los (Sweeney *theme tune*) De na na. De nana. De de de de dede de de de.

Frank exits. Los follows him out singing the Sweeney *theme tune, then re-enters laughing.*

Los A council place!

Harry Is there room for me?

Beat.

Los Oh Harry, oh, you know what, there's not, but fuck it. You wanna come, you can. It's only two bedrooms, the kids . . . Let me think . . .

Harry Forget it.

Pause.

Los That's one of the reasons we were hanging out for three bedrooms. But, you know, I can't hang on any longer, Harry . . .

Harry I don't want you to.

Los We've been living next to a prostitute, Harry. She's a drug addict. The kids fuckin' love her. And she's been great as a babysitter, she's saved my life. But she's not a great influence. We've got to get out of there.

Harry I know how you feel.

Pause.

Los We need a lottery win, don't we? If I had some money I'd buy a ticket. I feel lucky today. A pound. I've not even got a pound to spare. Just my luck. Today's the day I'd probably win but I've not even got the money for a ticket. (*Pause.*) Oh well. In one, Harry. In one.

Los downs her drink in one. Harry does likewise.

Drown your sorrows. That's my motto, drown 'em. Close your eyes and don't think of fuckin' England. Think of good times to come. The World Cup's this year. Terry thinks we might win it. He's had a bet on it. Dream, Harry. Live the fuckin' dream.

Harry rises to his feet and bursts into song. His gaze is distant. Eyes brim with tears.

Harry
Of all the money 'ere I had,
I spent it in good company.
And all the harm I've ever done,
Alas it was to none but me.
And all I've done for want of wit
To mem'ry now I can't recall,
So fill for me the parting glass
Good night and joy be with you all.

Los Aaah, that was lovely.

Harry I want you to sing it at my funeral.

Los Me?

Harry You will, won't you?

Beat.

Los If you want to go out to the sound of a strangled cat, of course I will.

Harry You sang it at your mam's wake. I'll never forget it.

Beat.

Los You're losing it again, Harry.

Harry What?

Los My mam's not dead, Harry. You think I'm Gracie again, don't you? I'm not Gracie, I'm Los, you silly sod.

Pause.

Harry Where's Gracie then?

Pause.

Los Er . . . She's, er . . . she's dead, Harry.

Harry What? She's dead?

Los Yeah, she er . . . a long time ago. You must remember, cancer. The boys were . . . well, they were just boys. Terry had to be the man, he bunked off school for the year to look after you, that's why he's so fuckin' thick. You drunk the Tyne dry, man. And then you went for the fuckin' Wear. But luckily it was full of shite, and it poisoned you, so you stopped.

Harry She's dead. (*He cries.*)

Los You need another drink.

Harry No. No, I, er . . . I want to be alone.

Beat.

Los Oh. Alright. Aah, sorry I . . . Well it's best to tell you the truth, isn't it? I didn't want to get your hopes up, did I, that any second now she'd walk through the door?

Harry No.

Los Right. Well I'll send wor Billy round later, check up on you. Oh, while I remember. The cheque. (*Takes a cheque book from her bag.*) Your signature.

She puts the cheque in front of him and gives him a pen.

Harry What's this for?

Los It's for Terry. His carer's pay.

Harry Oh. Oh yeah. (*Signs the cheque.*)

Los A new place, Harry. (*Sings.*) Celebrate good times, come on! De de de de de de de.

Harry That's great. I'm really pleased about that.

Los Aah. (*Hugs him.*) What year is it?

Harry 2010.

Los Who's Prime Minister?

Harry Gordon Brown.

Los Who's the Devil?

Harry Mike Ashley.

Los You've got it, Harry. You've still fuckin' got it. (*Exits.*)

Fade to black.

SCENE EIGHT

Spotlight on Harry. He's in his vest and pyjama bottoms, 'away with the fairies', laughing his head off. He suddenly assumes a character. He pretends to have a cigarette in his mouth and he peruses the audience as Bobby Thompson, 'The Little Waster'.

Harry Thank you. Ee, I've had a look around here tonight. I bet there's some debt in here. With your debt and my debt we'd pay Freddie Laker's debt off. I'm not laughing. I cannot sleep for debt. I'm up to here – (*His forehead.*) I wish I was a bit taller. You believe Bobby Thompson. If you pay what you owe, you'll never gan out. We call it debt – others call it credit. Committee men's wives 'on account'. Yes, well, I'm in debt on account of not being able to pay my credit. Mind, I will say this, you get some funny dreams. I had an awful dream. Well it wasn't all awful, it was good in parts. I dreamed Margaret Thatcher had died. Ah – but she went to Heaven. Ah, but St Peter tell her, 'Get away, down with Nick.' She went down to Old Nick, 'Howay in, Maggie. Howay in.' – Ah, but he got fed up. He rung Peter, he says 'Peter, get this woman out of here. She's only been here three days and she's closed three furnaces' . . .

Terry (*voice only*) Dad. Dad. Dad! It's me, Terry. It's Terry, Dad.

*Harry looks around, the lights on the room come up
and the spotlight goes off. The room is a bomb site.
The chair and the two-seat sofa have been turned over.
The coffee table has been smashed and broken. Photos
and memorabilia from the old home are scattered.
A pair of Harry's trousers are on the floor. Terry stands
a few feet away from Harry.*

It's okay, Dad. It's me, Dad. It's me, Terry. It's Terry, Dad.

Harry scrutinises Terry's face.

Harry Terry?

Terry What the fuck's happened here?

Harry Terry?

Terry Don't tell me you've been robbed?

Harry When did you get so old?

Terry What?

Harry How did you get so old?

Pause.

Terry You. You've fuckin' aged me. I've aged about three
hundred years caring for you.

Harry It's my fault, is it?

Terry Did you do this? Or were you robbed? (*Pause.*)
You did it, didn't you?

Harry What?

Terry The thirty-minute fuckin' makeover. You did it?

Harry looks at the state of the room.

Harry What?

Terry I can't be doing this. I've got a pick-up in ten
minutes.

Harry You've always got a pick-up in ten minutes.

Terry Yeah, well . . . ten minutes, twenty minutes, an hour. Time's money, that's the fuckin' thing. Time's money. And I've got none of fuckin' either

Harry If you were born today you'd be diagnosed with something.

Terry What?

Pause. Terry puts the chair back upright.

I'll make you a cup of tea to go with your sleeping pill.

Harry Have you seen your mam? Where is she?

Terry Yeah, yeah, yeah, I've seen her. She'll be back later.

Harry Oh good. At least I know she'll be back.

Terry turns the sofa back upright.

Terry Oh yeah, she'll be back. You can cuddle up and down a bottle of Southern Comfort, like the old days.

Harry Only Frank says you're taking the piss.

Pause.

Terry Well, he would, wouldn't he?

Harry Frank says she's dead and you're taking the piss.

Terry I'm not taking the fuckin' piss. I'm just . . . I'm just trying to keep you happy, that's all, Dad.

Harry You're trying to keep me happy?

Terry Yes, believe it or not.

Harry Oh, I believe it. I believe everything you tell me. Why wouldn't I?

Terry Alright then, have it Frank's way. She's dead, Dad. She died a very long time ago. And while I'm at it, here's a bit more bad news for you, Woolworth's is fuckin' dead too.

Harry I know she's dead! But where is she?

Pause.

Terry Sit down and I'll get your pill.

Harry I got the job.

Terry The job?

Harry At Leslie's. I got the job. Apprentice welder. I got the job.

Beat.

Terry Well done.

Harry I was scared stiff. But I did well in the interview. And I got the job.

Terry That's great, Dad. Fuckin' brilliant, man. Congratulations. Three sugars. No Alzheimer's coming up. (*Exits to kitchen.*)

Pause. Harry strains to remember something. It comes to him. Misty eyed, he recites with glee a long-remembered poem, 'Autobiography', by Jack Davitt, the Shipyard Poet.
Halfway through Terry enters with a mug of tea and sleeping pill. He stops and watches Harry finish.

Terry Sleeping pill, Dad.

Harry turns and looks at Terry who tries to give him the mug of tea.

Harry I'm losing my mind.

Terry No, no, you're just . . . you're just like . . . Yeah, you are, you've already lost it.

Harry One minute I've got it. And a second later it's gone. I don't know where it is. I've lost it.

Terry I wish I could lose my mind. Life would be a lot easier, I tell you. I'd love to lose my mind. Doing my fuckin' head in, it is.

Harry You haven't got much of a mind to lose.

Pause.

Terry I should've stayed at school. I might've . . . I could've been . . . I could've done . . . I could've been . . .

Harry A contender?

Terry I could've gone to university.

Harry You could've gone to university?

Terry I could've done. If I'd've stayed at school. Who knows?

Harry I dropped you on your head once, when you were a bairn. I've always wondered.

Terry Were you blethered?

Harry No, no. No I wasn't blethered. I was . . . stoned. I was stoned.

Terry You're fuckin' joking?

Harry Well, it was the sixties, weren't it? Even in Hebburn. John Lennon got me into it.

Terry Oh, right.

Harry Tune in. Drop out. I never did. I should've done. I wanted to. But it passed me by. I wish I hadn't worked so hard. I wish I'd spent more time with my Gracie and the bairns. I wish I'd allowed myself to be happier.

Terry Tea, Dad. Tea. Pill.

Harry Woolworth's is dead? Did you say Woolworth's is dead?

Terry Yeah, Woolworth's is gone, Dad. Along with the shipyards, the pits, and now the fuckin' quangos. But it's all looking up cos they've opened a New Bank. The Metro Bank. So we'll all be fine. Open up.

Harry All the rubbish we used to buy in Woolie's. D'you remember? All the rubbish we bought you in that place just to keep you happy. It never worked. All the shite, and the pick'n'mix, and still it wasn't enough. And now you're telling me it's gone. Woolworth's is dead.

Terry Yeah, Woolworth's is dead.

Harry Unbelievable.

Terry Pill, Dad. Open up.

He tries to give the tea and pill to Harry, who knocks them away across the room.

Harry I don't want a sleeping pill! I don't want your drugs! (*Turns the chair over.*) You think I don't know what you're up to? You think I don't know what you want?

Terry I don't know what I fuckin' want. So how the fuck you know what I want is beyond me.

Harry You know what you want.

Terry What? What do I want?

Pause.

Harry What?

Pause.

Terry What do I fuckin' want?

Pause.

Harry I don't know.

Terry Oh fuckin' hell. I can't . . . This is . . . I've got a fuckin' pick-up in ten minutes!

Harry You've always got a pick-up in ten minutes.

Terry Oh my God! Oh my God! Help me, God! Please help me, God! Please, please help me! I can't fuckin' cope. Please, Lord Jesus, please, please help me.

Frank and Susan enter.

Frank What's going on?

Harry He's cracking up. I knew he would one day.

Terry I resign! I fuckin' . . . I resign! I can't fuckin' care for him no more! I just can't!

Harry He's gonna need a carer if he's not careful.

Susan Are you okay, Harry?

Harry Me? Aye, I'm fine. I've had a good day. I got that job.

Frank Job?

Terry At Leslie's. He got the job at Leslie's. Apprentice welder.

Harry I did a very good interview. They really liked me.

Beat.

Frank Oh . . . well done, Dad.

Terry He needs professional help. It's a home, isn't it? He needs a fuckin' home.

Susan What's happened here? It's like a bomb site.

Frank We've had the upstairs tenant on the phone, complaining about thuds and shouts.

Terry You should've seen it when I walked in. I thought he'd been robbed.

Harry I have been robbed.

Terry You what?

Harry Two boys.

Terry I fuckin' knew it! Bastards! Robbin' an old man. They should be fuckin' shot!

Frank Is this true? What did they look like?

Harry You. They looked like you. They looked exactly like you two. I gave them everything they wanted. I didn't fight. I let them have it.

Pause.

Terry I told you, he's lost it. Gobbledee-fuckin'-gook.

Susan Sit down, Harry. I'll make you a cup of tea.

He tries to sit Harry down.

Terry It's a home, innit? He needs a fuckin' home.

Los marches in.

Los How much longer are you gonna be? We're gonna be late.

Harry Gracie.

Los Alright, Harry?

Terry Yeah, yeah, let's go. You sort this out. I've got to get out of here.

Frank Where you going?

Terry *The Last Airbender.*

Frank Well, we can't stay. We're off on holiday tomorrow. We're in the middle of packing.

Harry Are you going on holiday?

Frank We told you.

Terry You said nothing to us. Who's gonna look after him?

Frank You are. You're his fucking carer.

Terry Not any more I'm not. I fuckin' resigned.

Harry You're not Gracie.

Los No, Harry. Los, I'm fuckin' Los.

Harry Where's Gracie?

Terry For fuck sake! Sleeping pill! Someone give him a sleeping pill!

Harry I don't want a fucking sleeping pill! And I don't want to sit in this fucking chair! (*Gets up.*) I want my old chair! I want my old green fucking chair! And I don't want to stay here! I want to go home! I want to go home!

Pause.

Frank We sold it, Dad. You can't go back.

Harry I know we sold it. Can't we buy it back? You're goin' on holiday. Things must be lookin' up again.

Susan It's a cheap holiday, Harry. Only Greece. They're in terrible debt. Southern Europe's a financial basket case. We're just taking advantage.

Frank Kids go free, Dad.

Harry Who bought it?

Susan A young family. A lovely, lovely young family.

Terry Fuckin' Tories, Dad.

Los They had a poster up in your window during the election, Harry.

94

Terry I nearly put a fuckin' brick through it, didn't I?

Frank We haven't got the money, Dad. We can't buy it back.

Pause.

Harry I want my sleeping pill.

Terry At last. I'll get it.

Terry exits to kitchen. Harry sits.

Los What you like? (*The memorabilia on the floor.*) You been playing happy families again?

Susan Tidy-up time, I think. Tidy-up time.

Frank I'll put some of those pictures up. (*Exits to hall.*)

Susan and Los begin tidying up.

Los So how long are you going for, Sue?

Susan A fortnight.

Terry enters with a sleeping pill and a glass of water.

Terry A fortnight? Fuckin' hell! A fortnight!

Los Alright for some.

Frank enters with a toolbox.

Frank Well, two weeks cost virtually the same as one.

Terry All down to me then, is it? As usual.

Frank As usual?

Terry Yes. As usual. I'll be here four times a fuckin' day. What about Anya? She'll have fuck-all to do. Can she help out?

Susan Anya's coming with.

Terry She's what?

Frank We need a rest. We're exhausted.

Susan Training as a marriage counsellor is a lot harder than you could ever imagine.

Terry It's a lot easier than cabbing and looking after an old man whose brain's fuckin' gone.

Los D'you need someone else to help wipe the bairns' arses? I'll come.

Terry Aye, count us in. I'm good with a fuckin' toilet roll and spoilt brats, me.

Frank Well, at least they're not brainless psychopaths.

Los Wor Billy's not brainless. He's top of the fuckin' class.

Terry That's right. He's really fuckin' clever. I dunno where he gets it from.

Los He'll outstrip your two, no matter how much money you spend on them.

Terry Yeah. Ritalin. Fuckin' Ritalin, that is.

Los It's turned him into a genius.

Terry I've tried it. Doesn't work for me. But him, Einstein, man. Fuckin' Einstein.

Harry It breaks my heart.

They all look at Harry who is very emotional.

It breaks my heart. The banks of the Tyne. There's imported coal piled high on the banks of the Tyne. They've bought it in from the former Soviet Union where miners are working in conditions we fought to get rid of in the nineteenth century. It breaks my heart.

Terry Sleeping pill, Dad. Open Sesame, come on, sleeping pill.

Beat.

Frank Take your pill, Dad. A good night's sleep and you'll wake up fresh as a daisy.

Susan Absolutely, that's exactly what you need, Harry. Bye-byes. Take your pill and have a lovely deep bye-byes.

Los Harry, take your pill, darlin'.

Harry Gracie?

Los Aye, it's me. Take your pill, my love.

Beat.

Harry I'll take it off you.

Harry opens his mouth. Terry gives Los the pill and she pops it in Harry's mouth. Harry washes it down with water. Pause.

Terry Right. *Last Airbender.* Let's go.

Los What's the point? We've missed the beginning.

Terry It's about *The Last Airbender*. And he has to find all the other fuckin' benders. What else d'you want to know?

Frank I think you're right about a home. (*Pause.*) When we get back we should, er . . . talk about it.

Pause.

Terry Yeah, I know. Yeah.

Los It's a shame, poor old sod. But it's right.

Susan Absolutely. It's . . . well . . . it's coming to us all.

Frank The good ones cost an arm and a leg.

Susan Daylight robbery.

Terry I know. And the council ones are . . .

Los Scary . . .

Pause.
Harry sings the theme from D:Ream, 'Things Can Only Get Better' . . .
Pause.

Terry Come on.

Los and Terry exit.

Frank I'll help you into bed, shall I, Dad?

Harry I can put myself to bed.

Pause.

Susan Well, I'll get your PJs then. At least you'll be in your PJs.

Harry Stop fussin'. I'm not a bairn. Off you go. Leave me alone. I want to be alone. And I want my music on. I want my music.

Frank Yeah, of course, Dad. What d'you want on, Dad?

Harry It's in there. I've been trying to work it all day.

Frank switches the TV onto the AV channel and turns on the CD player.

Susan D'you know what I'm going to get you, Harry? I'm going to get you an iPod. From the airport. You'll have it when we get back. A little pressie.

The music plays. Louis Armstrong, 'It's a Wonderful World'.

Frank Satchmo. I might have known. Satchmo. He'll sort you out, Dad.

They all listen to the music.

Susan Louis Armstrong. Wow. Louis Armstrong.

Harry Off you go. Go on. Go.

Pause. Frank places the remote next to Harry.

Frank Love you, Dad.

Susan Yeah, me too, Harry. I love you too.

Pause. They exit. The front door opens and closes shut behind them. Pause. Harry shifts his position and accidentally knocks the remote onto the floor. The channel switches, the music goes off and the TV back on.

Harry Shit! No! No!

Harry looks down and picks up the remote. He tries to switch back to the AV channel but gets a news channel. And then another news channel. A film. A steamy sex scene. A shopping channel. MTV. Rap music. Bloomberg. Financial charts. The stock market. More sex. A murder. The channel-hopping gets faster. Harry works himself into a frenzy. The channels hop faster and faster.

I'm goin' home! To my house! That's my house! Not this house! I'm goin' home!

Harry throws the remotes to the floor and leaves. The front door opens and slams shut. The AV channel comes back on. Music: it's still Louis Armstrong, 'It's a Wonderful World'.

Fade to black.

SCENE NINE

The next morning. The curtains are open, daylight floods in, casting shadows from the bars on the window across the room. Frank sits in the armchair. Susan is on her mobile.

Susan Recently refurbished, one bedroom, en suite bathroom, living room stroke kitchenette. Suitable for, er . . .

Frank A first foot on the ladder.

Susan A first foot on the ladder . . . £49,000.

Frank £49,995.

Susan £49,995.

Frank Have you said the area's on the up again?

Susan I've said that.

Frank nods yes.

Any spark of interest latch on, we just want rid of it . . .

The front door opens and bangs shut. Terry enters followed by Los.

Terry What's happenin'? Have they found him?

Long pause.

Frank He's dead. (*Pause.*) Hypothermia. He, er . . . he was found in Hodgkin Park. In his underpants. A woman walking her dog.

Terry launches himself at Frank, knocking him to the floor. Frank does his best to protect himself as Terry pummels him with both fists.

Los Terry!

Susan Get off him!

Terry Happy? Happy are you? Fuckin' happy? Are you fuckin' happy?

Los Terry!

Terry stops punching.

Terry You killed him. You know that, don't you. Stickin' him here. You might as well have got a gun. Bang-bang.

Frank And you! Look in the fuckin' mirror!

Terry I know! I know! I know! I know!

Pause. Terry gets off Frank. Susan immediately goes to comfort him.

Frank It's okay. I'm fine.

He gets up.

We've got to go and identify the body.

Terry You mean it might not be him?

Frank No. It's, er . . . well I gave him a necklace with a tag on it, his address and telephone number.

Terry Like a fuckin' dog?

Los Stop it! Leave it, Terry! It's not his fault. It's no one's fault. No one's to blame. We've all done our best. We couldn't have done any more. It's a shit fuckin' world. And now we need to stick together. That's what Harry would've wanted. Wouldn't he?

Susan She's right. You're right, Los. That is what Harry would have wanted.

Los We're family. Blood is thicker than fuckin' water. Who'll look out for you when it comes to it? Family. Who'll be there when no one else's interested? Family.

Who'll be there at your deathbed? Fuckin' family, that's who. You might not want 'em there but they'll fuckin' well be there. So just . . . we have to pull together.

Susan I agree.

Pause.

Los Right. There's phone calls to make. Shall we split them, Sue?

Susan Absolutely.

Terry We can't use our phone, we've been cut off. Incoming calls only.

Susan The office. Come on, Los. We'll use my office phones.

Pause. Susan hugs Frank. Los hugs Terry. Susan hugs Terry. Los hugs Frank. Susan and Los hug. It's all very emotional.

Right.

Susan and Los exit. Pause. Terry reaches out and hugs Frank. Frank responds. They hug each other tight until Frank taps Terry's back and Terry lets go. Pause.

Frank Shall we go and identify him then?

Terry No, no, no. I coudn't. I just, you know, the er . . . the fuckin' Joker out of *Batman* thing, I just couldn't. I don't want to be haunted.

Frank A bit late for that. (*Pause.*) It's hard, isn't it? It's so hard to do the right thing. The way things are organised, this society, the pressure, the way we treat old people . . . Or is it? Is that just an excuse? Because we know really, we know, in our hearts, we know when we're not . . . doing the right thing. 'Treat others as you would want to be treated yourself.' That was his favourite saying, weren't it? He must have said it to us a thousand times when we were kids. And then he stopped. He could see it hadn't gone in and he gave up. It's only sitting here this morning that I've understood it in all its fullness. Well, I'm going to live by it from now on. I'm going to take up the torch. And do my best to pass it on to my kids.

Terry Yeah, me too. I'm gonna do that. For Dad, yeah. Treat others as you would want to be treated yourself.

Pause. Frank exits. The front door slams shut. Terry breaks down. It's primal. As he sobs he picks up Harry's trousers from the floor. He takes the wallet from the trouser pocket, opens it and, still sobbing, steals Harry's last twenty pounds.

Slow fade to black.